Number Primer

This edition published 2025
by Living Book Press
Copyright © Living Book Press, 2025

ISBN: 978-1-922919-46-5 (hardcover)
        978-1-922919-45-8 (softcover)

First published in 1909.

All rights reserved. No part of this publication may be reproduced, stored in a retrieval system, or transmitted in any other form or means – electronic, mechanical, photocopying, recording or otherwise, without the prior permission of the copyright owner and the publisher or as provided by Australian law.

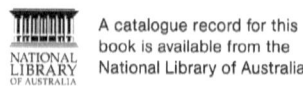

A catalogue record for this book is available from the National Library of Australia

Arithmetic Primer

by

BAILEY & GERMANN

PART I

Numbers through Nine	11–19	**Addition — 1's**	
Numbers through Nineteen		Combinations Developed	27–29
Counting	20	Chart	30
Reading	21	Table	31
		Combinations	32
Measurements		Oral Problems	33
Pint and Quart	22		
Dime, Nickel,		**Addition — 2's**	
and Cent	23	Combinations Developed	34–36
Numbers through Ninety-nine		Chart	37
Counting by 10's	24	Table	38
Recognition of Groups	25	Combinations	39
Reading	26	Oral Problems	40

PART II

Addition — 1's		Decreasing Numbers of Two	
Table	41	Orders	54
Increasing Numbers of		Written Examples	55
Two Orders	42		
		Addition — 3's	
Subtraction — 1's		Combinations with	
Development	43	Objects	56
Combinations	44	Table	57
Oral Problems	45	Combinations	58
Decreasing Numbers of Two		Oral Problems	59
Orders	46	Increasing Numbers of Two	
		Orders	60
		Counting by 3's	61
Addition — 2's		Problems	
Table	47	(Counting by 3's)	62
Increasing Numbers of Two		Written Examples	67
Orders	48		
Counting by 2's	49	**Subtraction — 3's**	
Problems		Development	63
(Counting by 2's)	50	Combinations	64
Written Examples	55	Oral Problems	65
		Decreasing Numbers of Two	
Subtraction — 2's		Orders	66
Development	51	Written Examples	67
Combinations	52		
Oral Problems	53		

Buying and Selling	
Making Change	68, 69
Measurements	
Foot	70
Inch	71
Dozen	72
Problems	72
Comparisons	73
Addition — 4's	
Combinations with Objects	74
Table	75
Combinations	76
Oral Problems	77
Increasing Numbers of Two Orders	78
Counting by 4's	79
Problems (Counting by 4's)	80
Written Examples	85

Subtraction — 4's	
Development	81
Combinations	82
Oral Problems	83
Decreasing Numbers of Two Orders	84
Written Examples	85
Miscellaneous	
Problems solved with Objects	86, 87
Written Problems in Addition and Subtraction	88, 89
Addition Combinations of 2's, 3's, and 4's	90
Subtraction Combinations of 2's, 3's, and 4's	91
Increasing Numbers of Two Orders by 2's, 3's, and 4's	92
Decreasing Numbers of Two Orders by 2's, 3's, and 4's	93
Writing Numbers	94

PART III

Numbers through Nine hundred inety-nine — Reading	95
Roman Numerals through XII	96
Addition — 5's	
Combinations with Objects	97
Table	98
Combinations	99
Oral Problems	100
Increasing Numbers of Two Orders	101
Counting by 5's	102
Problems (Counting by 5's)	103
Written Examples	110
Subtraction — 5's	
Development	106
Combinations	107

Oral Problems	108
Decreasing Numbers of Two Orders	109
Written Examples	110
Objective Solutions	104, 105
Fractions	
Halves and Fourths	111
Thirds and Sixths	116
Naming Parts	117
Problems	118
Measurements	
Telling Time to Quarter Hour	112
Parts of a Dollar	113
Buying and Selling	
Making Change	114, 115

Addition — 6's	
Combinations with	
Objects	119
Table	120
Combinations	121
Oral Problems	122
Increasing Numbers of Two	
Orders	123
Problems	
(Adding by 6's)	124
Written Examples	129
Subtraction — 6's	
Development	125
Combinations	126
Oral Problems	127
Decreasing Numbers of Two	
Orders	128
Written Examples	129
Addition — 7's	
Combinations with	
Objects	130
Table	131
Combinations	132
Oral Problems	133
Increasing Numbers of Two	
Orders	134
Problems	
(Adding by 7's)	135
Written Examples	140
Subtraction — 7's	
Development	136
Combinations	137
Oral Problems	138
Decreasing Numbers of Two	
Orders	139
Written Examples	140
Addition — 8's	
Combinations with	
Objects	141
Table	142
Combinations	143
Oral Problems	144
Increasing Numbers of Two	
Orders	145
Problems	
(Adding by 8's)	147
Written Examples	152
Subtraction — 8's	
Development	148
Combinations	149
Oral Problems	150
Decreasing Numbers of Two	
Orders	151
Written Examples	152
Measurements	
Quart and Peck	146
Review Problems	153
Comparisons	154, 155
Addition — 9's	
Combinations with	
Objects	156
Table	157
Combinations	158
Oral Problems	159
Increasing Numbers of Two	
Orders	160
Problems	
(Adding by 9's)	161
Written Examples	166
Subtraction — 9's	
Development	162
Combinations	163
Oral Problems	164
Decreasing Numbers of Two	
Orders	165
Written Examples	166
Miscellaneous	
Written Problems	
(Addition and Subtraction)	167-172
Fundamental Combinations	73, 174
Vocabulary	175, 176

PREFACE

THIS primer renders available for the use of pupils beginning the study of number a series of exercises that deal primarily with the fundamental combinations in addition and subtraction and their application. In form and substance these exercises are simple, progressive, and within the reading experience of pupils. The exercises are the outgrowth of three years' classroom experimentation in the selection and arrangement of number material adapted to the needs and understanding of first and second year pupils. The text has been so designed that it may be placed in the pupils' hands as soon as they have acquired the simple vocabulary of the first exercise, during the second week in school. The use of this book necessitates the same guidance as is given with the use of a supplementary primer or first reader. The text supplements the teacher's oral development, includes the essential drill exercises in compact form, and offers the pupils opportunity to visualize number relations. The book is divided into three parts, each of which covers approximately the ground for one half-year's work.

Part I supplies the essential material for the first half-year, presented in picture and simple story form. The exercises of the first half-year, which must necessarily be mainly oral and objective, relate to simple problems of the child's daily experience and to measuring with the units illustrated in the text, and include the addition combinations of numbers of one order with 1 and 2.

Part II covers the ground of the second half-year's work. The exercises of this part are principally occupied with the addition combinations of numbers of one order with 1, 2, 3, and 4, and their correlated subtraction combinations, and with the application of these combinations to the increasing and decreasing of numbers of two orders.

Part III treats of the work of the third half-year. The exercises of this part bring to a logical completion the groundwork of the primer. They deal primarily with the addition combinations of numbers of one order with 5, 6, 7, 8, and 9, and their correlated subtraction combinations, and with the application of these combinations to the increasing and decreasing of numbers of two orders.

Parts II and III contain, in addition to the groundwork enumerated, exercises illustrative of the application of counting and addition to the solution of easy problems of the multiplication and division types, and exercises dealing with measures and simple comparisons..

The problem exercises have been carefully planned as to vocabulary and scope. The vocabulary (pp. 176, 176) consists of 376 words distributed as follows: Part I, 67 words; Part II, 203 new words; Part III, 106 new words. A few of the words are easy technical terms; the others are such as may be found in the usual primers and first readers. With the necessary drill preliminary to a new reading exercise, and with preparatory work of a nature similar to the printed problems, pupils can read and interpret the exercises of the text. The reading and solution of number stories develop a sense of power and independence, and offer a means for the correlation of reading with number work.

The following are the special features of this book: the adaptation of number exercises, both as to substance and as to mode of expression, to the understanding of pupils at the very beginning of number work; the selection of graphic illustrations that elucidate the purpose of the exercises illustrated; the development of the fundamental addition and subtraction combinations from concrete representations, abundant drill on these combinations in abstract form, and their application to easy concrete oral problems; the orderly development of exercises dealing with the increasing and decreasing of numbers of two orders by numbers of one order, as a preparation for column addition and for subtraction; and finally, a logical arrangement of the exercises, which answers the requirements of a good teaching sequence.

SUGGESTIONS TO TEACHERS

THE oral work to accompany Part I should include, in addition to the exercises suggested by the text, simple problems dealing with the four fundamental operations, whose solution can be easily determined with the use of objects.* When a pupil has mastered number concepts up to ten, for example, he is prepared to solve problems of the following types by counting objects one at a time.

ADDITION. There are 3 apples on one plate and 2 apples on another plate. How many apples are there on both plates?
Solution. The pupil puts 3 splints in one group and 2 splints in another group, and counts the splints.

SUBTRACTION. There were 5 cups on the table. 2 cups were taken away. How many cups remained on the table?
Solution. The pupil puts 5 splints in a group, takes 2 of them away, and counts the splints that remain.

MULTIPLICATION. John plants 4 trees in a row. He plants 2 rows of trees. How many trees does he plant?
Solution. The pupil places 4 splints in each of 2 groups, and counts the splints.

DIVISION. (Measuring.) I give 8 cents to some boys. To each boy I give 2 cents. How many boys receive money from me?
Solution. The pupil takes 8 splints, gives 2 splints to each of several boys in succession, and counts the number of boys who receive splints.

DIVISION. (Partition.) I give 6 marbles to 3 boys. To each boy I give the same number of marbles. How many marbles does each boy receive?
Solution. The pupil takes 6 splints, distributes them one at a time in rotation among 3 boys, and counts the number received by one boy.

As the pupil learns the addition and subtraction combinations of Parts II and III, he is prepared for column addition and for subtraction, and for the more expeditious solution of simple problems related to the five types noted. The advance of Parts II and III over Part I is illustrated by the following methods of solution of the first three problems just mentioned:

ADDITION. The pupil applies the combination 3 + 2, and finds the answer 5 from this relation.

SUBTRACTION. The pupil applies the combination 5 - 2, and finds the answer 3 from this relation.

MULTIPLICATION. The pupil applies counting by 4's, and from the relation 4 and 4 are 8, finds the answer.

In teaching the combinations the aim should be to have each combination in addition associated with its sum, and each combination in subtraction with its remainder. The association should be direct and immediate. It is an error to have constant reference to objects for the purpose of correcting mistakes made by the pupils. After the combinations have been objectively developed, pupils should be required to memorize them in tabular form. Mistakes in the statement of the results of the combinations are best corrected by having the pupil repeat the table involved. The tables are memorized with ease, because the sums have the common difference of one. The laws of association are followed, because the terms to be associated and their result are brought into direct and immediate relation. The combinations are not properly known, however, until the pupil can give the results as readily as he is required to recognize a printed word. To encourage direct association, it is well to require the pupil to name, both in concert work and in individual recitation, the results of a series of miscellaneous combinations, such as row 6 of Exercise 44, without a pause, and at the uniform rate of two a second, as indicated by the tapping of a pencil.

For the purpose of relating the combinations dealing with increasing and decreasing numbers of two orders by numbers of one order, with their correlated fundamental combinations, the first column of exercises similar to Exercises 28 and 82 includes the latter combinations..

Attention is called to the Arabic figures occurring instead of dots in the rectangles of exercises similar to Exercise 42. This is a typographic device to indicate the fact that the combinations which these figures represent have occurred in preceding exercises. The small full-faced figures in the addition tables of exercises similar to Exercise 43 indicate the same fact.

For training in thought and expression, pupils may be required to formulate questions whose substance is suggested by the elliptical statements occurring in exercises similar to Exercise 48, or whose numerical terms are indicated by the incomplete equations of exercises similar to Exercises 48 and 60.

Variety in sequence will be obtained in the use of drill exercises on the combinations, if exercises similar to Exercises 44, 46, 50, and 52 are read forwards and backwards by rows, and up and down by columns.

PART I

NUMBERS THROUGH NINE

EXERCISE 1. — THE NUMBER ONE

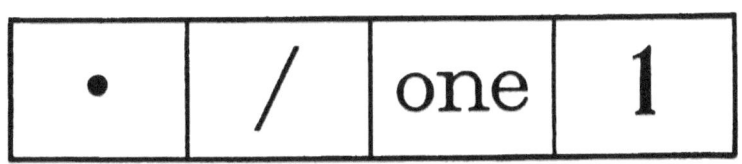

I see

I see

You see

I see

You see

You see

NUMBERS THROUGH NINE

EXERCISE 2. — THE NUMBER TWO

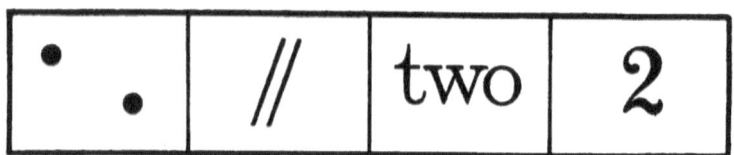

I have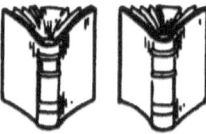

I have

You have

I see

You have

You see

NUMBERS THROUGH NINE

EXERCISE 3. — THE NUMBER THREE

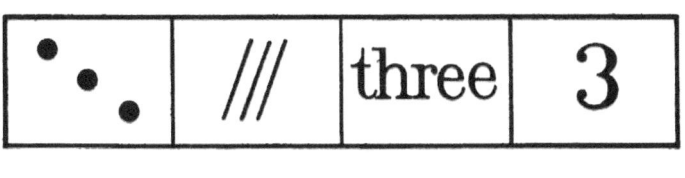

You have

You see

You see

I have

I see

I see

EXERCISE 4. — THE NUMBER FOUR

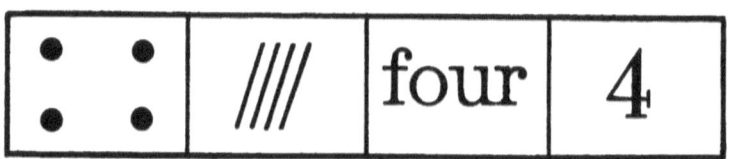

I see

I have

I have

You have

You see

You see

NUMBERS THROUGH NINE

EXERCISE 5. — THE NUMBER FIVE

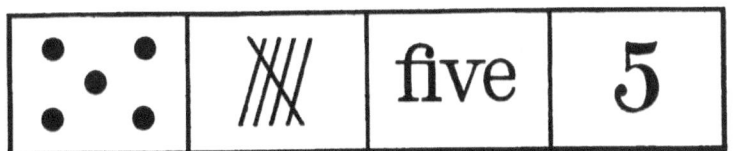

Jack sees

Jack sees

Jack has

You have

I have

I see

NUMBERS THROUGH NINE

EXERCISE 6. — THE NUMBER SIX

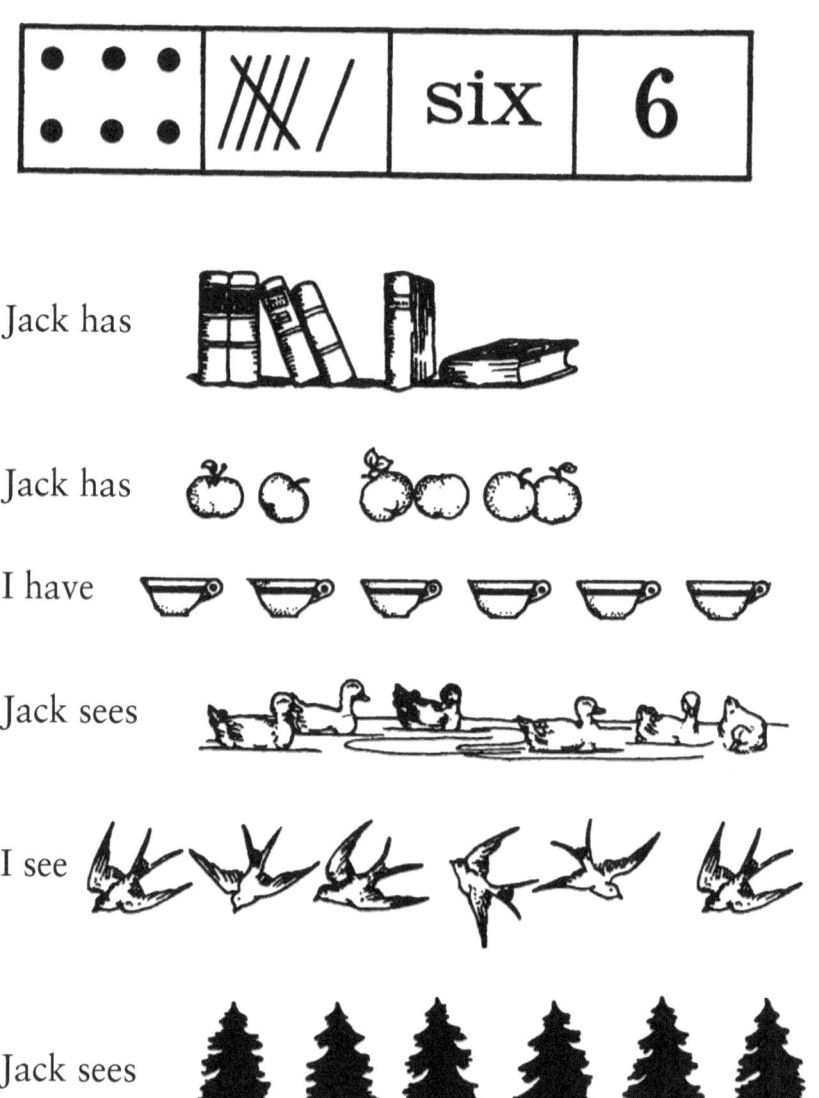

Jack has

Jack has

I have

Jack sees

I see

Jack sees

EXERCISE 7. — THE NUMBER SEVEN

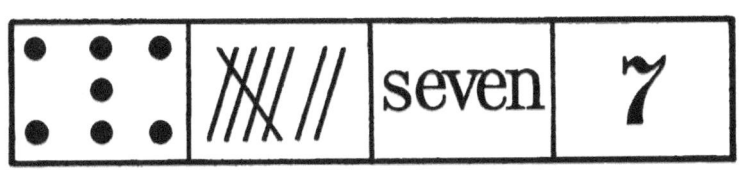

I have

Jack has

I see

You see

You have

Jack sees

EXERCISE 8. — THE NUMBER EIGHT

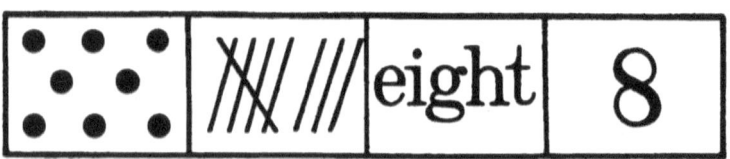

Jack has

I see

You have

You see

I see

Jack sees

NUMBERS THROUGH NINE

EXERCISE 9. — THE NUMBER NINE

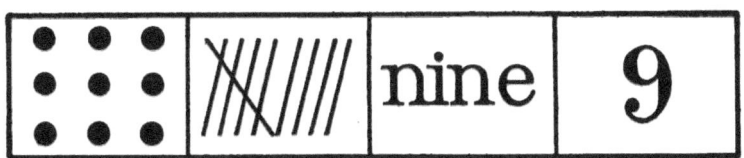

Jack sees

I have

You see

Jack has

You see

Jack sees

EXERCISE 10. — COUNTING

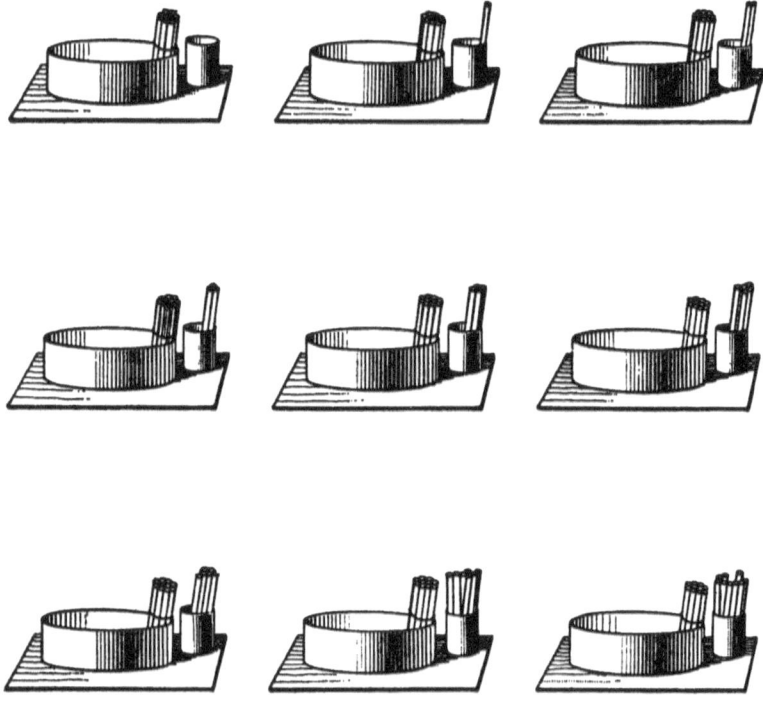

NOTE. Pupil reads: "Ten, ten-one, ten-two, ten-nine;" and then, "Ten, eleven, twelve,... nineteen."

NUMBERS THROUGH NINETEEN

EXERCISE 11. — READING NUMBERS

8	18	2	12	4
19	2	11	16	10
0	9	18	3	13
6	16	5	15	7
12	2	9	19	8
17	7	16	6	3
5	11	13	0	1
15	19	16	13	6
4	14	11	10	15

MEASUREMENTS

EXERCISE 12. — PINT AND QUART

2 pints are 1 quart

MEASUREMENTS

EXERCISE 13. — DIME, NICKEL, CENT

EXERCISE 14. — COUNTING BY TENS

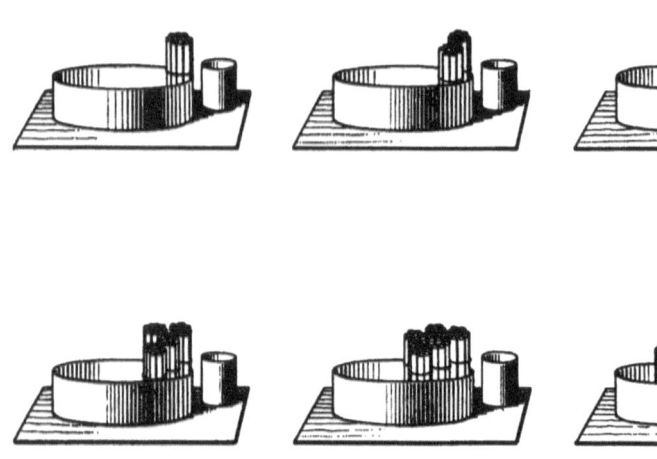

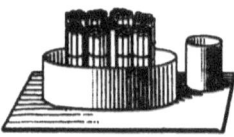

NOTE. Pupil reads: "One ten, two tens,... nine tens;" and then, "Ten, twenty,... ninety." Pupil counts dimes in the same way.

NUMBERS THROUGH NINETY-NINE

EXERCISE 15. — RECOGNITION OF GROUPS

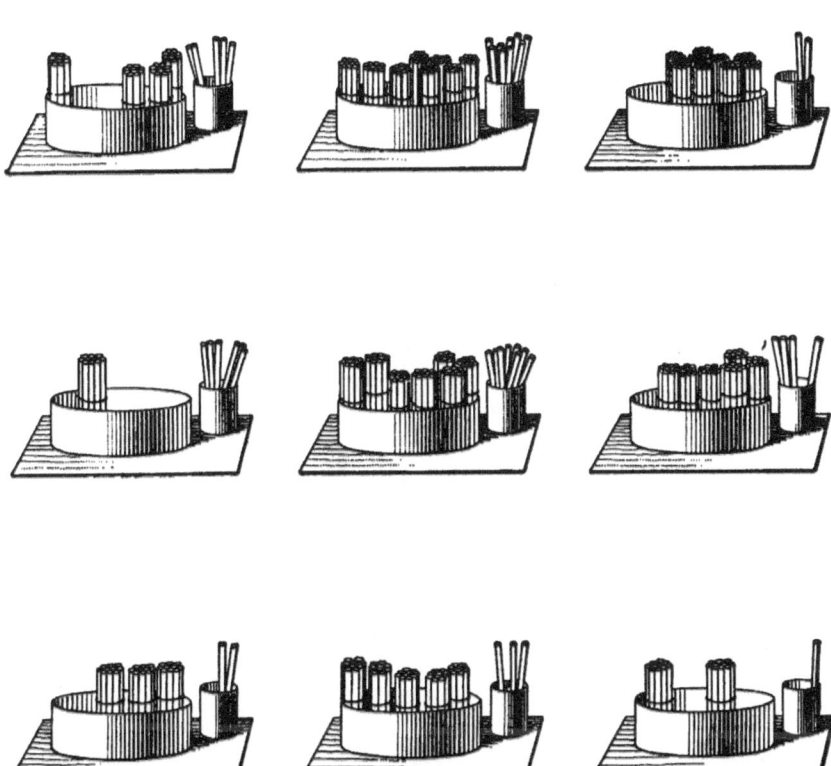

NOTE. Pupil reads: "Four tens five units, eight tens nine units, two tens one unit;" then "Forty-five, eighty-nine,... twenty-one."

NUMBERS THROUGH NINETY-NINE

EXERCISE 16. — READING NUMBERS

54 87 20 63 42

75 39 96 57 69

46 28 77 84 95

68 59 86 25 44

99 62 48 73 51

27 35 64 92 49

56 65 74 47 67

43 34 83 38 22

55 88 97 79 58

ADDITION — 1'S

EXERCISE 17. — COMBINATIONS

1 and 1 are —

2 and 1 are —   1 and 2 are —

3 and 1 are —   1 and 3 are —

EXERCISE 17.— COMBINATIONS (CONTINUED)

4 and 1 are —   1 and 4 are —

5 and 1 are —   1 and 5 are —

6 and 1 are —   1 and 6 are —

ADDITION — 1'S

EXERCISE 17.— COMBINATIONS (CONTINUED)

7 and 1 are — 1 and 7 are —

8 and 1 are — 1 and 8 are —

9 and 1 are — 1 and 9 are —

ADDITION — 1'S

EXERCISE 18. — THE COMBINATIONS WITH OBJECTS

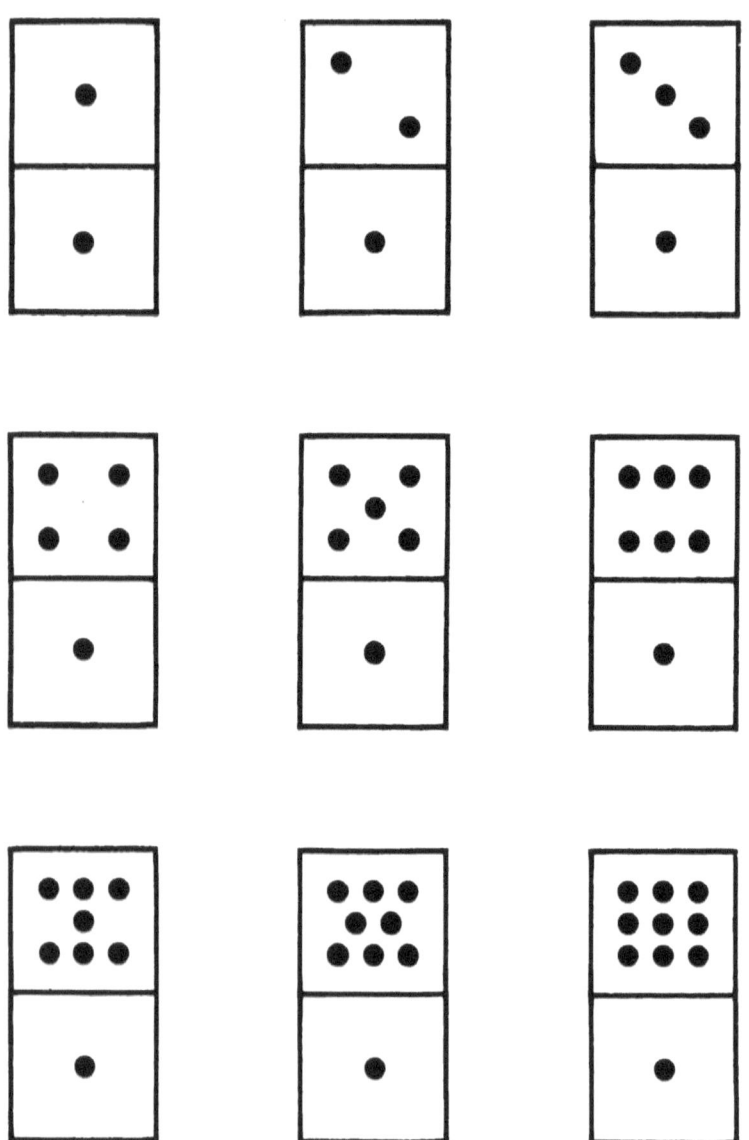

ADDITION — 1'S

EXERCISE 19. — TABLE

1 and 1 are —	1 and 1 are —
2 and 1 are —	1 and 2 are —
3 and 1 are —	1 and 3 are —
4 and 1 are —	1 and 4 are —
5 and 1 are —	1 and 5 are —
6 and 1 are —	1 and 6 are —
7 and 1 are —	1 and 7 are —
8 and 1 are —	1 and 8 are —
9 and 1 are —	1 and 9 are —
0 and 1 are —	1 and 0 are —

ADDITION — 1'S

EXERCISE 20. — THE COMBINATIONS

1. 1 2 3 4 5 6 7 8 9 0
    1 1 1 1 1 1 1 1 1 1

2. 1 1 1 1 1 1 1 1 1 1
    1 2 3 4 5 6 7 8 9 0

3. 3 7 0 2 8 1 4 9 6 5
    1 1 1 1 1 1 1 1 1 1

4. 1 1 1 1 1 1 1 1 1 1
    0 5 8 4 2 6 3 1 9 7

5. 1 9 1 7 1 4 1 3 1 2
    7 1 3 1 1 1 9 1 5 1

6. 5 1 0 1 8 1 6 1 1 9
    1 4 1 0 1 2 1 8 6 1

ADDITION — 1'S

EXERCISE 21. — ORAL PROBLEMS

1. Jack has one apple. I have three apples. We have — apples.

2. We see 1 cat. We see 5 more cats. We see — cats.

3. Ned gives me 1 leaf. Jack gives me 7 leaves. I then have — leaves.

4. May brings me 1 cup. She brings me 4 more cups. She brings me — cups.

5. A man has 1 pig. He buys 9 more pigs. He then has — pigs.

6. There are 8 sheep in the lot. 1 more comes in. How many sheep are now in the lot?

7. Jack eats 1 apple. Ned eats 2 apples. They eat — apples.

8. Jack has 1 can of water. Jill has 6 cans of water. How many cans of water have they?

9. Ned sold 7 sheep. Then he sold 1 sheep. How many sheep did he sell?

ADDITION — 2'S

EXERCISE 22. — COMBINATIONS

2 and 2 are —

3 and 2 are —

2 and 3 are —

4 and 2 are —

2 and 4 are —

ADDITION — 2'S

EXERCISE 22. — COMBINATIONS (CONTINUED)

5 and 2 are —   2 and 5 are —

6 and 2 are —   2 and 6 are —

7 and 2 are —   2 and 7 are —

ADDITION — 2'S

EXERCISE 22. — COMBINATIONS (CONTINUED)

8 and 2 are —   2 and 8 are —

9 and 2 are —   2 and 9 are —

ADDITION — 2'S

EXERCISE 23. — THE COMBINATIONS WITH OBJECTS

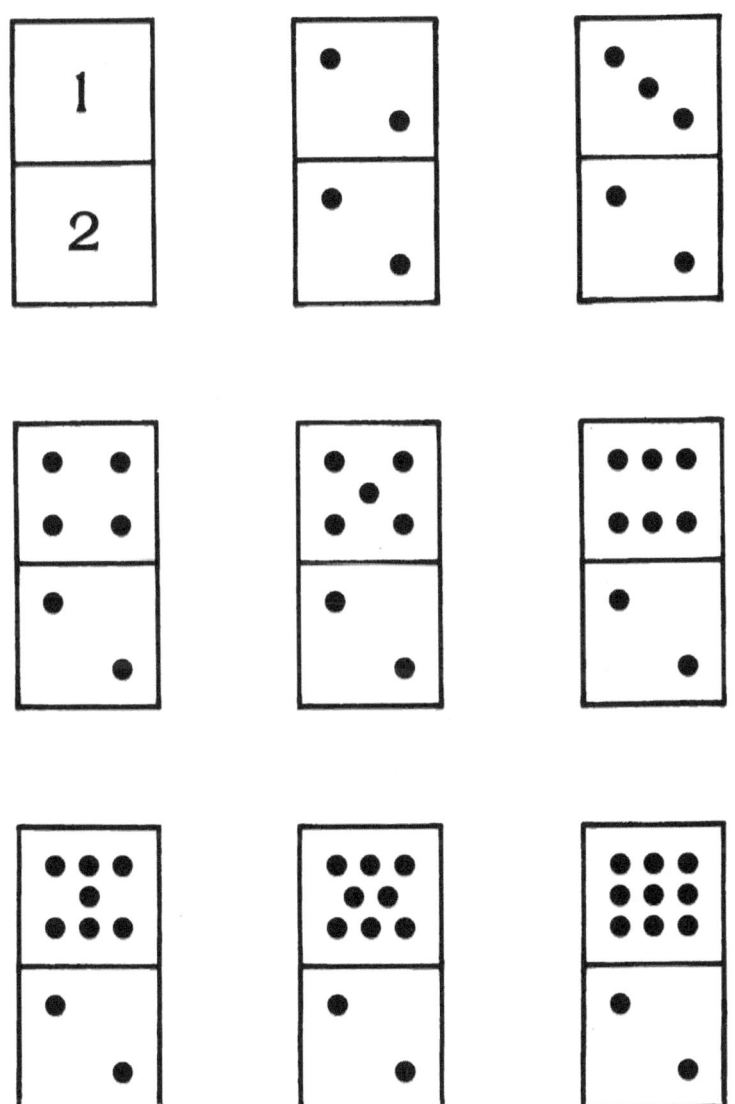

ADDITION — 2'S

EXERCISE 24. — TABLE

1 and 2 are—	2 and 1 are —
2 and 2 are—	2 and 2 are —
3 and 2 are—	2 and 3 are —
4 and 2 are—	2 and 4 are —
5 and 2 are—	2 and 5 are —
6 and 2 are—	2 and 6 are —
7 and 2 are—	2 and 7 are —
8 and 2 are—	2 and 8 are —
9 and 2 are—	2 and 9 are —
0 and 2 are—	2 and 0 are —

ADDITION — 2'S

EXERCISE 25. — THE COMBINATIONS

1. $\frac{1}{2}$ $\frac{2}{2}$ $\frac{3}{2}$ $\frac{4}{2}$ $\frac{5}{2}$ $\frac{6}{2}$ $\frac{7}{2}$ $\frac{8}{2}$ $\frac{9}{2}$ $\frac{0}{2}$

2. $\frac{2}{1}$ $\frac{2}{2}$ $\frac{2}{3}$ $\frac{2}{4}$ $\frac{2}{5}$ $\frac{2}{6}$ $\frac{2}{7}$ $\frac{2}{8}$ $\frac{2}{9}$ $\frac{2}{0}$

3. $\frac{8}{2}$ $\frac{5}{2}$ $\frac{1}{2}$ $\frac{3}{2}$ $\frac{0}{2}$ $\frac{7}{2}$ $\frac{9}{2}$ $\frac{2}{2}$ $\frac{4}{2}$ $\frac{6}{2}$

4. $\frac{2}{0}$ $\frac{2}{4}$ $\frac{2}{9}$ $\frac{2}{6}$ $\frac{2}{1}$ $\frac{2}{3}$ $\frac{2}{7}$ $\frac{2}{5}$ $\frac{2}{2}$ $\frac{2}{8}$

5. $\frac{6}{2}$ $\frac{2}{3}$ $\frac{8}{2}$ $\frac{2}{2}$ $\frac{2}{8}$ $\frac{1}{2}$ $\frac{2}{4}$ $\frac{7}{2}$ $\frac{2}{0}$ $\frac{4}{2}$

6. $\frac{2}{5}$ $\frac{9}{2}$ $\frac{2}{7}$ $\frac{5}{2}$ $\frac{2}{9}$ $\frac{3}{2}$ $\frac{2}{6}$ $\frac{0}{2}$ $\frac{2}{1}$ $\frac{8}{2}$

ADDITION — 2'S

EXERCISE 26. — ORAL PROBLEMS

1. A man sold 2 sheep. Then he sold 6 sheep. He sold — sheep.

2. The cow eats 8 apples. The sheep eats 2 apples. They eat — apples.

3. I have 2 cups. You have 4 cups. We have — cups.

4. I see 9 pigs. 2 more pigs come. I now see — pigs.

6. May has 2 books. I give her 7 books. She now has — books.

6. Jack has 2 books. Ned gives him 2 books. How many books does Jack then have?

7. May has 2 cups. Ann has 9 cups. How many cups have they?

8. Ned plays with 3 dogs. 2 more dogs come to play. Ned now plays with — dogs.

9. The sheep drinks 2 pints of water. The cow drinks 5 pints. They drink — pints of water.

PART II

ADDITION - 1'S

EXERCISE 27. — TABLE

1 + 1 =	7 + 1 =	1 + 3 =	1 + 9 =
6 + 1 =	1 + 2 =	1 + 8 =	5 + 1 =
1 + 1 =	1 + 7 =	4 + 1 =	0 + 1 =
1 + 6 =	3 + 1 =	9 + 1 =	1 + 5 =
2 + 1 =	8 + 1 =	1 + 4 =	1 + 0 =

1. 1 cent and 7 cents are — cents.
2. 6 cows and 1 cow are — cows.
3. 1 boy and 9 boys are — boys.
4. 8 cats and 1 cat are — cats.

5. 1 + 6 =	3 + 1 =	1 + 8 =	1 + 4 =
6. 1 + 0 =	1 + 5 =	0 + 1 =	5 + 1 =
7. 7 + 1 =	6 + 1 =	1 + 2 =	1 + 9 =
8. 1 + 3 =	8 + 1 =	4 + 1 =	9 + 1 =
9. 1 + 1 =	1 + 7 =	2 + 1 =	1 + 1 =

ADDITION — 1'S

EXERCISE 28. — INCREASING NUMBERS OF TWO ORDERS

1.	1 _1_	11 _1_	21 _1_	31 _1_	41 _1_	80 _1_	60 _1_	90 _1_
2.	2 _1_	12 _1_	22 _1_	42 _1_	13 _1_	93 _1_	73 _1_	53 _1_
3.	4 _1_	14 _1_	24 _1_	34 _1_	44 _1_	94 _1_	74 _1_	84 _1_
4.	5 _1_	15 _1_	35 _1_	55 _1_	85 _1_	75 _1_	65 _1_	25 _1_
5.	6 _1_	16 _1_	26 _1_	46 _1_	36 _1_	86 _1_	56 _1_	66 _1_
6.	7 _1_	17 _1_	37 _1_	57 _1_	77 _1_	97 _1_	27 _1_	47 _1_
7.	8 _1_	18 _1_	28 _1_	48 _1_	68 _1_	88 _1_	98 _1_	78 _1_
8.	9 _1_	19 _1_	49 _1_	79 _1_	29 _1_	59 _1_	89 _1_	39 _1_

SUBTRACTION — 1'S

EXERCISE 29. — DEVELOPMENT

1 + ? = 2
How many are 2 - 1?

1 + ? = 2
How many are 2 - 1?

1 + ? = 3
How many are 3 - 1?

2 + ? = 3
How many are 3 - 2?

1 + ? = 4
How many are 4 - 1?

3 + ? = 4
How many are 4 - 3?

1 + ? = 5
How many are 5 - 1?

4 + ? = 5
How many are 5 - 4?

1 + ? = 6
How many are 6 - 1?

5 + ? = 6
How many are 6 - 5?

1 + ? = 7
How many are 7 - 1?

6 + ? = 7
How many are 7 - 6?

1 + ? = 8
How many are 8 - 1?

7 + ? = 8
How many are 8 - 7?

1 + ? = 9
How many are 9 - 1?

8 + ? = 9
How many are 9 - 8?

1 + ? = 10
How many are 10 - 1?

9 + ? = 10
How many are 10 - 9?

SUBTRACTION — 1'S

EXERCISE 30. — THE COMBINATIONS

1. 3 4 5 6 7 8 9 10
   −1 −1 −1 −1 −1 −1 −1 −1

2. 3 4 5 6 7 8 9 10
   −2 −3 −4 −5 −6 −7 −8 −9

3. 8 6 4 9 7 5 1 10
   −1 −1 −1 −1 −1 −1 −1 −1

4. 7 4 6 3 8 1 9 10
   −6 −3 −5 −2 −7 −0 −8 −9

5. 9 5 8 3 7 4 6 10
   −1 −4 −1 −2 −6 −1 −5 −1

6. 8 9 2 7 4 6 5 10
   −1 −8 −1 −1 −3 −1 −4 −9

7. 9 - 1 =   6 - 1 =   8 - 7 =   10 - 9 =

8. 7 - 1 =   9 - 8 =   5 - 1 =   10 - 1 =

9. 5 - 4 =   7 - 6 =   8 - 1 =   6 - 5 =

SUBTRACTION — 1'S

EXERCISE 31. — ORAL PROBLEMS

1. Rose has 8 cents. She gives 1 cent to Ann. She then has — cents.

2. May has 7 roses. 1 of the roses is red. The other roses are white. She has — white roses.

3. This nest has 9 eggs. That nest has 8 eggs. This nest has — more egg than that nest.

4. Jack buys 4 books. Ned buys 3 books. Jack buys — more book than Ned.

5. A man has 7 sheep. He sells 6 sheep. He has — sheep left.

6. There were 5 birds in a tree. 4 of them flew away. How many birds were then in the tree?

7. Ned has 10 cents. He buys a book for 9 cents. He has — cent left.

8. Rose buys a book for 6 cents. She buys an apple for 5 cents. How much more does the book cost than the apple?

9. May buys 2 pints of milk. She drinks 1 pint. How many pints are left?

SUBTRACTION — 1'S

EXERCISE 32. — SUBTRACTING NUMBERS OF TWO ORDERS

1.	2 $\underline{1}$	12 $\underline{1}$	32 $\underline{1}$	62 $\underline{1}$	82 $\underline{1}$	91 $\underline{1}$	21 $\underline{1}$	41 $\underline{1}$
2.	3 $\underline{1}$	13 $\underline{1}$	23 $\underline{1}$	63 $\underline{1}$	14 $\underline{1}$	34 $\underline{1}$	54 $\underline{1}$	74 $\underline{1}$
3.	5 $\underline{1}$	15 $\underline{1}$	25 $\underline{1}$	85 $\underline{1}$	35 $\underline{1}$	55 $\underline{1}$	75 $\underline{1}$	95 $\underline{1}$
4.	6 $\underline{1}$	16 $\underline{1}$	26 $\underline{1}$	66 $\underline{1}$	46 $\underline{1}$	96 $\underline{1}$	56 $\underline{1}$	76 $\underline{1}$
5.	7 $\underline{1}$	17 $\underline{1}$	27 $\underline{1}$	47 $\underline{1}$	67 $\underline{1}$	57 $\underline{1}$	97 $\underline{1}$	37 $\underline{1}$
6.	8 $\underline{1}$	18 $\underline{1}$	28 $\underline{1}$	88 $\underline{1}$	78 $\underline{1}$	38 $\underline{1}$	58 $\underline{1}$	98 $\underline{1}$
7.	9 $\underline{1}$	19 $\underline{1}$	29 $\underline{1}$	49 $\underline{1}$	69 $\underline{1}$	99 $\underline{1}$	59 $\underline{1}$	39 $\underline{1}$
8.	10 $\underline{1}$	20 $\underline{1}$	30 $\underline{1}$	70 $\underline{1}$	50 $\underline{1}$	40 $\underline{1}$	90 $\underline{1}$	60 $\underline{1}$

ADDITION — 2'S

EXERCISE 33. — TABLE

1 + 2 =	6 + 2 =	2 + 1 =	2 + 6 =
2 + 2 =	7 + 2 =	2 + 2 =	2 + 7 =
3 + 2 =	8 + 2 =	2 + 3 =	2 + 8 =
4 + 2 =	9 + 2 =	2 + 4 =	2 + 9 =
5 + 2 =	0 + 2 =	2 + 5 =	2 + 0 =

1. 2 cups and 5 cups are — cups.
2. 9 dogs and 2 dogs are — dogs.
3. 2 books and 7 books are — books.
4. 6 boats and 2 boats are — boats.
5. 8 birds and 2 birds are — birds.

6. 4 + 2 =	5 + 2 =	2 + 1 =	9 + 2 =
7. 2 + 2 =	0 + 2 =	2 + 6 =	2 + 5 =
8. 2 + 9 =	2 + 3 =	2 + 2 =	2 + 0 =
9. 1 + 2 =	6 + 2 =	8 + 2 =	7 + 2 =
10. 2 + 7 =	2 + 8 =	3 + 2 =	2 + 4 =

ADDITION — 2'S

EXERCISE 34. — INCREASING NUMBERS OF TWO ORDERS

1. | 1 | 11 | 21 | 31 | 51 | 80 | 70 | 60 |
    | 2 | 2 | 2 | 2 | 2 | 2 | 2 | 2 |

2. | 2 | 12 | 32 | 62 | 13 | 93 | 23 | 43 |
    | 2 | 2 | 2 | 2 | 2 | 2 | 2 | 2 |

3. | 4 | 14 | 64 | 24 | 54 | 34 | 94 | 84 |
    | 2 | 2 | 2 | 2 | 2 | 2 | 2 | 2 |

4. | 5 | 15 | 45 | 85 | 95 | 55 | 35 | 25 |
    | 2 | 2 | 2 | 2 | 2 | 2 | 2 | 2 |

5. | 6 | 16 | 56 | 76 | 86 | 46 | 26 | 36 |
    | 2 | 2 | 2 | 2 | 2 | 2 | 2 | 2 |

6. | 7 | 17 | 67 | 87 | 97 | 57 | 37 | 47 |
    | 2 | 2 | 2 | 2 | 2 | 2 | 2 | 2 |

7. | 8 | 18 | 28 | 78 | 48 | 38 | 58 | 98 |
    | 2 | 2 | 2 | 2 | 2 | 2 | 2 | 2 |

8. | 9 | 19 | 49 | 99 | 69 | 59 | 79 | 89 |
    | 2 | 2 | 2 | 2 | 2 | 2 | 2 | 2 |

ADDITION — 2'S

EXERCISE 35. — COUNTING BY 2'S

1. Read the numbers in bold figures:

   1   **2**   3   **4**   5   **6**   7   **8**   9   **10**
11 **12** 13 **14** 15 **16** 17 **18** 19 **20**

2. Name the sums:

0 + 2,   2 + 2,   4 + 2,   6 + 2,   8 + 2,
10 + 2, 12 + 2, 14 + 2, 16 + 2, 18 + 2.

3. Count these dots by 2's:

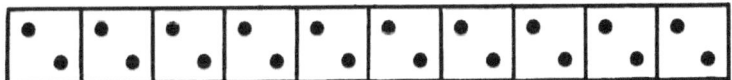

4. Count by 2's:

2,   2,   2,   2,   2,   2,   2,   2,   2,   2.

5. Find the sum of the 2's in each box:

| 2 2
2
2 2 | 2 2 2
2 2
2 2 2 | 2 2 2
2 2 2
2 2 2 | 2 2 2
2
2 2 2 | 2 2
2 2
2 2 |

ADDITION — 2'S

EXERCISE 36. — PROBLEMS (COUNTING BY 2'S)

1. 🍎🍎 🍎🍎 🍎🍎   Here are — apples. Two apples cost 1 cent. I pay — cents for all.

2. ○○○○○○○   Here are — cents. At 2 apples for 1 cent, I can buy — apples.

3. ⬜⬜⬜⬜   Here are — cans. Each can holds 2 pints. The cans hold — pints.

4. How many pints are there in 1 quart? How many pints are there in 8 quarts?

5. Jack has 3 boxes. Into each box he puts 2 dates. He has — dates in the 3 boxes.

6. May buys 9 pears. Each pear costs 2 cents. How much do the 9 pears cost?

SUBTRACTION — 2'S

EXERCISE 37. — DEVELOPMENT

2 + ? = 3
How many are 3 — 2?

1 + ? = 3
How many are 3 — 1?

2 + ? = 4
How many are 4 — 2?

2 + ? = 4
How many are 4 — 2?

2 + ? = 5
How many are 5 — 2?

3 + ? = 5
How many are 5 — 3?

2 + ? = 6
How many are 6 — 2?

4 + ? = 6
How many are 6 — 4?

2 + ? = 7
How many are 7 — 2?

5 + ? = 7
How many are 7 — 5?

2 + ? = 8
How many are 8 — 2?

6 + ? = 8
How many are 8 — 6?

2 + ? = 9
How many are 9 — 2?

7 + ? = 9
How many are 9 — 7?

2 + ? = 10
How many are 10 — 2?

8 + ? = 10
How many are 10 — 8?

2 + ? = 11
How many are 11 — 2?

9 + ? = 11
How many are 11 — 9?

SUBTRACTION — 2'S

EXERCISE 38. — THE COMBINATIONS

1.   4   5   6   7   8   9   10   11
     2   2   2   2   2   2   2   2

2.   4   5   6   7   8   9   10   11
     2   3   4   5   6   7   8   9

3.   9   7   10   8   6   4   11   2
     2   2   2   2   2   2   2   2

4.   8   10   9   11   5   7   2   3
     6   8   7   9   3   5   0   1

5.   6   11   7   9   10   5   3   8
     4   2   5   2   8   2   2   6

6.   8   4   5   11   6   9   7   10
     2   2   3   9   2   7   2   2

7. 11 - 2 =   7 - 5 =   6 - 2 =   9 - 7 =

8. 6 - 4 =   8 - 2 =   10 - 2 =   7 - 2 =

9. 11 - 9 =   10 - 8 =   8 - 6 =   9 - 2 =

SUBTRACTION — 2'S

EXERCISE 39. — ORAL PROBLEMS

1. Rob has a dime. He buys a book for 8 cents. He has — cents left.

2. There were 11 sheep in a lot. 9 sheep ran away. — sheep were left.

3. May is 8 years old. Rose is 2 years old. May is — years older than Rose.

4. May buys 9 cups. Rose buys 7 cups. May buys — more cups than Rose.

5. Jack brings 7 pails of water. Jill brings 2 pails of water. Jack brings — pails more than Jill.

6. Ned is 4 years old. In how many years will he be 6 years old?

7. On our street there are 2 dogs. On the next street there are 4 dogs. The next street has — more dogs than our street.

8. I buy a pencil for 2 cents. I pay for it with a dime. How many cents do I get back?

9. There are 11 boys and 2 girls in the room. How many more boys than girls are in the room?

SUBTRACTION — 2'S

EXERCISE 40. — DECREASING NUMBERS OF TWO ORDERS

1.	3 2	13 2	23 2	53 2	73 2	92 2	42 2	82 2
2.	4 2	14 2	24 2	64 2	15 2	45 2	55 2	95 2
3.	6 2	16 2	26 2	76 2	96 2	56 2	66 2	36 2
4.	7 2	17 2	27 2	87 2	37 2	67 2	77 2	47 2
5.	8 2	18 2	28 2	98 2	48 2	78 2	58 2	88 2
6.	9 2	19 2	29 2	59 2	79 2	49 2	89 2	39 2
7.	10 2	20 2	40 2	60 2	90 2	30 2	50 2	80 2
8.	11 2	21 2	31 2	61 2	81 2	41 2	71 2	51 2

ADDITION AND SUBTRACTION — 2'S

EXERCISE 41. — WRITTEN EXAMPLES

Add:

	(1)	(2)	(3)	(4)	(5)	(6)	(7)	(8)
	1	1	1	2	2	1	2	2
	1	1	2	2	1	1	2	2
	1	2	2	2	2	2	1	2
	2	2	2	2	2	2	2	2
A.	1	1	1	1	2	2	2	2

	(1)	(2)	(3)	(4)	(5)	(6)	(7)	(8)
	22	12	12	21	20	12	22	20
	20	13	20	20	22	23	22	10
	21	20	15	21	12	20	11	24
B.	12	22	22	27	22	22	22	22

	(1)	(2)	(3)	(4)	(5)	(6)	(7)	(8)
	20	12	22	10	12	21	12	21
	11	10	11	2	20	10	6	50
	12	20	10	11	10	7	30	2
	21	23	12	1	11	20	10	22
C.	22	11	2	22	22	11	11	2

Subtract:

	(1)	(2)	(3)	(4)	(5)	(6)	(7)	(8)
	48	87	63	79	34	56	94	42
D.	32	72	21	57	12	32	21	12

	(1)	(2)	(3)	(4)	(5)	(6)	(7)	(8)
	86	25	74	98	67	38	57	86
E.	62	23	22	76	42	16	52	66

ADDITION — 3'S

EXERCISE 42. — THE COMBINATIONS WITH OBJECTS

ADDITION — 3'S

EXERCISE 43. — TABLE

1 + 3 =	6 + 3 =	3 + 1 =	3 + 6 =
2 + 3 =	7 + 3 =	3 + 2 =	3 + 7 =
3 + 3 =	8 + 3 =	3 + 3 =	3 + 8 =
4 + 3 =	9 + 3 =	3 + 4 =	3 + 9 =
5 + 3 =	0 + 3 =	3 + 5 =	3 + 0 =

1. 5 pans and 3 pans are — pans.
2. 3 birds and 9 birds are — birds.
3. 6 quarts and 3 quarts are — quarts.
4. 3 eggs and 8 eggs are — eggs.
5. 7 dogs and 3 dogs are — dogs.

6.	3 + 7 =	5 + 3 =	9 + 3 =	5 + 3 =
7.	0 + 3 =	7 + 3 =	3 + 3 =	6 + 3 =
8.	3 + 4 =	3 + 6 =	2 + 3 =	3 + 8 =
9.	8 + 3 =	4 + 3 =	3 + 9 =	3 + 1 =
10.	3 + 2 =	1 + 3 =	3 + 0 =	3 + 3 =

ADDITION — 3'S

EXERCISE 44. — THE COMBINATIONS

1. $\underline{\dfrac{1}{3}}$ $\underline{\dfrac{2}{3}}$ $\underline{\dfrac{3}{3}}$ $\underline{\dfrac{4}{3}}$ $\underline{\dfrac{5}{3}}$ $\underline{\dfrac{6}{3}}$ $\underline{\dfrac{7}{3}}$ $\underline{\dfrac{8}{3}}$ $\underline{\dfrac{9}{3}}$ $\underline{\dfrac{0}{3}}$

2. $\underline{\dfrac{3}{1}}$ $\underline{\dfrac{3}{2}}$ $\underline{\dfrac{3}{3}}$ $\underline{\dfrac{3}{4}}$ $\underline{\dfrac{3}{5}}$ $\underline{\dfrac{3}{6}}$ $\underline{\dfrac{3}{7}}$ $\underline{\dfrac{3}{8}}$ $\underline{\dfrac{3}{9}}$ $\underline{\dfrac{3}{0}}$

3. $\underline{\dfrac{6}{3}}$ $\underline{\dfrac{9}{3}}$ $\underline{\dfrac{7}{3}}$ $\underline{\dfrac{5}{3}}$ $\underline{\dfrac{0}{3}}$ $\underline{\dfrac{1}{3}}$ $\underline{\dfrac{4}{3}}$ $\underline{\dfrac{2}{3}}$ $\underline{\dfrac{3}{3}}$ $\underline{\dfrac{8}{3}}$

4. $\underline{\dfrac{3}{8}}$ $\underline{\dfrac{3}{3}}$ $\underline{\dfrac{3}{2}}$ $\underline{\dfrac{3}{6}}$ $\underline{\dfrac{3}{9}}$ $\underline{\dfrac{3}{7}}$ $\underline{\dfrac{3}{1}}$ $\underline{\dfrac{3}{0}}$ $\underline{\dfrac{3}{5}}$ $\underline{\dfrac{3}{4}}$

5. $\underline{\dfrac{5}{3}}$ $\underline{\dfrac{3}{4}}$ $\underline{\dfrac{2}{3}}$ $\underline{\dfrac{3}{1}}$ $\underline{\dfrac{7}{3}}$ $\underline{\dfrac{3}{9}}$ $\underline{\dfrac{6}{3}}$ $\underline{\dfrac{3}{3}}$ $\underline{\dfrac{8}{3}}$ $\underline{\dfrac{3}{0}}$

6. $\underline{\dfrac{9}{5}}$ $\underline{\dfrac{3}{2}}$ $\underline{\dfrac{0}{3}}$ $\underline{\dfrac{3}{7}}$ $\underline{\dfrac{4}{3}}$ $\underline{\dfrac{3}{5}}$ $\underline{\dfrac{1}{3}}$ $\underline{\dfrac{3}{8}}$ $\underline{\dfrac{7}{3}}$ $\underline{\dfrac{3}{6}}$

7. 3 and what other number will make each of these numbers: 12; 6; 10; 9; 3; 7; 4; 8; 5; 11?

ADDITION — 3'S

EXERCISE 45. — ORAL PROBLEMS

1. There are 3 eggs in one nest and 7 eggs in another nest. There are — eggs in the nests.

2. May has 5 white roses and 3 red roses. She has — roses.

3. Jack had 3 pencils. Rob gave him 6 more pencils. He then had — pencils.

4. In one lot there are 8 sheep. In another lot there are 3 sheep. There are — sheep in all.

6. There were 4 birds in a tree. 3 more birds came. There were then — birds in the tree.

6. Jack buys a pad for 3 cents and a pencil for 2 cents. How much do they cost?

7. I paid 3 cents for milk. I had 8 cents left. How many cents did I have at first?

8. The cup cost 9 cents. The plate cost 3 cents more. How much did the plate cost?

9. I buy two pencils. Each pencil costs 3 cents. How much do I pay for both?

ADDITION — 3'S

EXERCISE 46. — INCREASING NUMBERS OF TWO ORDERS

1.	1 3	11 3	21 3	61 3	31 3	80 3	40 3	50 3
2.	2 3	12 3	42 3	82 3	13 3	23 3	63 3	73 3
3.	4 3	14 3	54 3	94 3	64 3	74 3	84 3	44 3
4.	5 3	15 3	65 3	85 3	25 2	45 3	75 3	35 3
5.	6 3	16 3	26 3	96 3	76 3	46 3	66 3	36 3
6.	7 3	17 3	27 3	57 3	97 3	77 3	47 3	67 3
7.	8 3	18 3	28 3	68 3	88 3	58 3	98 3	78 3
8.	9 3	19 3	29 3	49 3	69 3	89 3	39 3	59 3

ADDITION — 3'S

EXERCISE 47. — COUNTING BY 3'S

1. Bead the numbers in bold figures:

1, 2, **3,** 4, 5, **6,** 7, 8, **9,** 10, 11, **12,** 13, 14, **15,** 16, 17, **18,** 19, 20, **21,** 22, 23, **24,** 25, 26, **27,** 28, 29, **30.**

2. Name the sums:

0 + 3,   3 + 3,   6 + 3,   9 + 3,   12+3,
15 + 3,   18 + 3,   21 + 3,   24 + 3,   27 + 3.

3. Count these dots by 3's:

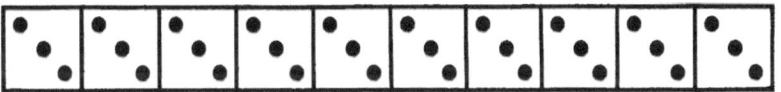

4. Count by 3's:

3, 3, 3, 3, 3, 3, 3, 3, 3, 3.

5. Find the sum of the 3's in each box:

3 3 3	3 3	3 3 3	3 3	3 3 3
3 3	3	3	3 3	3 3 3
3 3 3	3 3	3 3 3	3 3	3 3 3

ADDITION — 3'S

EXERCISE 48. — PROBLEMS (COUNTING BY 3'S)

1. ⋮ ⋮ ⋮ ⋮ ⋮ ⋮ Here are — marbles. At 3 for 1 cent, they cost — cents.

2. ○○○○○ Here are — cents. At 3 marbles for 1 cent, I can buy — marbles.

3. ✏✏✏✏✏✏ At 3¢ each these — pencils will cost — cents.

4. I have 12¢. If one pencil costs 3¢, I can buy — pencils.

5. I have 3 trains. On each train I have 3 cars. I have — cars on the 3 trains.

6. Jack buys 4 tops. Each top costs 3 cents. How much does he pay for all?

SUBTRACTION — 3'S

EXERCISE 49. — DEVELOPMENT

3 + ? = 4   1 + ? = 4
How many are 4 — 3?   How many are 4 — 1?

3 + ? = 5   2 + ? = 5
How many are 5 — 3?   How many are 5 — 2?

3 + ? = 6   3 + ? = 6
How many are 6 — 3?   How many are 6 — 3?

3 + ? = 7   4 + ? = 7
How many are 7 — 3?   How many are 7 — 4?

3 + ? = 8   5 + ? = 8
How many are 8 — 3?   How many are 8 — 5?

3 + ? = 9   6 + ? = 9
How many are 9 — 3?   How many are 9 — 6?

3 + ? = 10   7 + ? = 10
How many are 10 — 3? How many are 10 — 7?

3 + ? = 11   8 + ? = 11
How many are 11 — 3? How many are 11 — 8?

3 + ? = 12   9 + ? = 12
How many are 12 — 3? How many are 12 — 9?

SUBTRACTION — 3'S

EXERCISE 50. — THE COMBINATIONS

1. $\quad\underline{\begin{array}{c}5\\3\end{array}}\quad\underline{\begin{array}{c}6\\3\end{array}}\quad\underline{\begin{array}{c}7\\3\end{array}}\quad\underline{\begin{array}{c}8\\3\end{array}}\quad\underline{\begin{array}{c}9\\3\end{array}}\quad\underline{\begin{array}{c}10\\3\end{array}}\quad\underline{\begin{array}{c}11\\3\end{array}}\quad\underline{\begin{array}{c}12\\3\end{array}}$

2. $\quad\underline{\begin{array}{c}5\\2\end{array}}\quad\underline{\begin{array}{c}6\\3\end{array}}\quad\underline{\begin{array}{c}7\\4\end{array}}\quad\underline{\begin{array}{c}8\\5\end{array}}\quad\underline{\begin{array}{c}9\\6\end{array}}\quad\underline{\begin{array}{c}10\\7\end{array}}\quad\underline{\begin{array}{c}11\\8\end{array}}\quad\underline{\begin{array}{c}12\\9\end{array}}$

3. $\quad\underline{\begin{array}{c}9\\3\end{array}}\quad\underline{\begin{array}{c}7\\3\end{array}}\quad\underline{\begin{array}{c}11\\3\end{array}}\quad\underline{\begin{array}{c}8\\3\end{array}}\quad\underline{\begin{array}{c}4\\3\end{array}}\quad\underline{\begin{array}{c}12\\3\end{array}}\quad\underline{\begin{array}{c}3\\3\end{array}}\quad\underline{\begin{array}{c}10\\3\end{array}}$

4. $\quad\underline{\begin{array}{c}7\\4\end{array}}\quad\underline{\begin{array}{c}10\\7\end{array}}\quad\underline{\begin{array}{c}8\\5\end{array}}\quad\underline{\begin{array}{c}12\\9\end{array}}\quad\underline{\begin{array}{c}9\\6\end{array}}\quad\underline{\begin{array}{c}4\\1\end{array}}\quad\underline{\begin{array}{c}3\\0\end{array}}\quad\underline{\begin{array}{c}11\\8\end{array}}$

5. $\quad\underline{\begin{array}{c}12\\9\end{array}}\quad\underline{\begin{array}{c}9\\3\end{array}}\quad\underline{\begin{array}{c}6\\3\end{array}}\quad\underline{\begin{array}{c}3\\3\end{array}}\quad\underline{\begin{array}{c}11\\8\end{array}}\quad\underline{\begin{array}{c}10\\3\end{array}}\quad\underline{\begin{array}{c}7\\4\end{array}}\quad\underline{\begin{array}{c}5\\2\end{array}}$

6. $\quad\underline{\begin{array}{c}8\\3\end{array}}\quad\underline{\begin{array}{c}5\\3\end{array}}\quad\underline{\begin{array}{c}9\\6\end{array}}\quad\underline{\begin{array}{c}7\\3\end{array}}\quad\underline{\begin{array}{c}10\\7\end{array}}\quad\underline{\begin{array}{c}11\\3\end{array}}\quad\underline{\begin{array}{c}12\\3\end{array}}\quad\underline{\begin{array}{c}8\\5\end{array}}$

7. $\quad 10 - 3 = \qquad 7 - 4 = \qquad 12 - 9 = \qquad 11 - 3 =$
8. $\quad 9 - 6 = \qquad 12 - 3 = \qquad 9 - 3 = \qquad 8 - 3 =$
9. $\quad 8 - 5 = \qquad 10 - 7 = \qquad 7 - 3 = \qquad 11 - 8 =$

SUBTRACTION — 3'S

EXERCISE 51. — ORAL PROBLEMS

1. Ned is 7 years old. His sister is 3 years younger. His sister is — years old.

2. There are 8 trees on our street. There are 5 trees on the next street. On our street there are — more trees than on the next street.

3. Ned buys an apple for 3 cents. He pays for it with a nickel. He gets — cents back.

4. That can holds 4 pints. This can holds 7 pints. This can holds — more pints than that can.

6. Bob has a dime. He buys bread for 7 cents. How much money has he left?

6. A man has 11 sheep. He sells 8 of them. How many sheep has he left?

7. May is 3 years old. In how many years will she be 12 years old?

8. One day 6 boys and 9 girls were late. How many more girls than boys were late?

9. Mr. May has 6 sheep. 3 of them are white. The others are black. How many of them are black?

SUBTRACTION — 3'S

EXERCISE 52. — DECREASING NUMBERS OF TWO ORDERS

1. 4   14   24   44   64   83   53   33
    3   3   3   3   3   3   3   3

2. 5   15   25   65   16   36   76   56
    3   3   3   3   3   3   3   3

3. 7   17   27   57   87   47   97   67
    3   3   3   3   3   3   3   3

4. 8   18   28   88   48   98   68   78
    3   3   3   3   2   3   3   3

5. 9   19   29   49   99   69   79   39
    3   3   3   3   3   3   3   3

6. 10 20   30   90   60   70   50   80
    3   3   3   3   3   3   3   3

7. 11 21   31   61   71   51   81   41
    3   3   3   3   3   3   3   3

8. 12 22   32   72   52   82   42   92
    3   3   3   3   3   3   3   3

ADDITION AND SUBTRACTION — 3'S

EXERCISE 53. — WRITTEN EXAMPLES

Add:

	(1)	(2)	(3)	(4)	(5)	(6)	(7)	(8)
	1	1	3	3	2	2	3	2
	1	3	2	3	0	3	1	3
	3	3	2	3	3	2	1	0
	2	2	3	3	1	3	3	1
A.	3	3	3	3	3	2	3	3

	(1)	(2)	(3)	(4)	(5)	(6)	(7)	(8)
	23	30	11	21	31	30	13	33
	31	23	21	13	10	23	10	20
	13	13	32	12	32	12	31	11
B.	22	33	13	30	23	21	32	10

	(1)	(2)	(3)	(4)	(5)	(6)	(7)	(8)
	32	32	31	20	11	41	21	30
	13	2	2	32	31	2	30	5
	23	1	13	3	2	25	7	30
	10	22	1	12	23	10	10	2
C.	21	20	20	2	10	1	31	21

Subtract:

	(1)	(2)	(3)	(4)	(5)	(6)	(7)	(8)
	37	98	75	84	42	69	26	50
D.	34	13	22	51	30	36	23	20

	(1)	(2)	(3)	(4)	(5)	(6)	(7)	(8)
	43	71	29	55	86	95	68	59
E.	30	41	23	32	52	23	53	37

BUYING AND SELLING

EXERCISE 54. — MAKING CHANGE

1. May buys some bread for 6 cents. She pays for it with a dime. Please make the change.

2. I buy an apple for 2¢. I pay for it with a nickel. You may give me the change.

3. Jack pays for a 5¢ loaf of bread with a dime. Please make the change.

4. Please let me have nickels in change for a dime.

6. I wish to buy some bread for 5¢ and some milk for 8¢. You may give me the money to pay for them.

6. Please change this dime. You may give me a nickel and — cents.

7. How many dimes can I get for 4 nickels?

BUYING AND SELLING

8. I owe you 3 cents. Here is a dime. You may give me a nickel and — cents.

9. Rose wishes to buy a 13¢ book. She has a dime. How many more cents does she need?

10. Ann buys a 6¢ cake. She pays for it with a dime. She receives — cents in change.

11. Will buys a pencil for 3¢. He pays for it with a dime. You may make the change.

12. Rose pays with a dime for 5¢ worth of milk. She gets — cents in change.

13. Jack rides on the car. He pays his fare with a dime. He receives — cents in change.

14. Ned has 4 cents. He wishes to buy a 10¢ cake. He needs — cents more.

15. I pay for a 7¢ melon with a dime. You may give me the change.

NOTE. In making change it is customary for the dealer to name the price of the article sold, to add by 1's until a multiple of 5 is reached, and then to add by multiples of 5 until the amount given in payment is named. For example, problem 1 is solved by the pupil as follows: He takes the dime, he names the price 6¢, then gives in change 1¢, 1¢, 1¢ and 1¢, saying "7¢, 8¢, 9¢, 10¢."

DEFINITE MESAUREMENTS

EXERCISE 55. — FOOT

Walk along the front of the room from wall to wall. How many steps do you take? Do all the boys and girls take the same number of steps?

Walk along the side of the room from the front to the back. How many steps do you take? Count the number of steps taken by the others. Do they all take the same number of steps?

Now take a foot rule. Are all foot rules of the same size? Find how wide the room is. Find how long it is. How wide is your desk? How long is it? How high is it?

DEFINITE MESAUREMENTS

EXERCISE 56. — INCH

We use a rule one foot long to find the length of large things, such as the length of the room.

We use a shorter strip than the foot rule to find the size of small things.

A strip as long as this is *one inch long*.

Cut a strip of paper one inch long. With this find how many inches long the foot rule is.

12 inches are 1 foot.

Find how many inches long your hand is. How long is your book? How wide is it? How long is your pencil?

DEFINITE MESAUREMENTS

EXERCISE 57. — DOZEN

How many are 9 and 3? How many are 4 and 8? 10 and 2 are how many? 11 and 1 are how many?

We call 12 things by the name *dozen*.

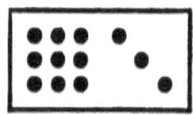 12 *things are one dozen.*

ORAL PROBLEMS

1. How many inches are one dozen inches?

2. How many eggs are one dozen eggs?

3. How many apples are one dozen apples?

4. Jack finds one dozen eggs in a nest. He sells 4 of them. How many eggs are left?

5. May buys one dozen pencils. 3 of them are red. The others are black. How many are black?

6. The can is 11 inches high. The cup is 3 inches high. How much higher is the can than the cup?

7. The red pole is 9 feet high. The white pole is 3 feet higher. How high is the white pole?

COMPARISONS

EXERCISE 58. — HOW MUCH LONGER OR SHORTER

1. Find how many inches long the line A is.

2. How long is the line D?

3. How long is the line B?

4. How long is the line C?

5. How much longer is the line A than the line B?

6. How many inches longer is the line C than the line D?

7. How long is the line E?

8. How long is the line F?

9. How much longer is the line F than the line E?

10. Which is the shorter, the line F or the line D? How much shorter?

11. Which is the shorter, the line C or the line F? How much?

12. How much longer is the line A than the line D?

ADDITION — 4'S

EXERCISE 59. — THE COMBINATIONS WITH OBJECTS

ADDITION — 4'S

EXERCISE 60. — TABLE

1 + 4 =	6 + 4 =	4 + 1 =	4 + 6 =
2 + 4 =	7 + 4 =	4 + 2 =	4 + 7 =
3 + 4 =	8 + 4 =	4 + 3 =	4 + 8 =
4 + 4 =	9 + 4 =	4 + 4 =	4 + 9 =
5 + 4 =	0 + 4 =	4 + 5 =	4 + 0 =

1. 4 dimes and 9 dimes are — dimes.
2. 6 trees and 4 trees are — trees.
3. 4 roses and 8 roses are — roses.
4. 5 feet and 4 feet are — feet.
5. 4 pints and 7 pints are — pints.

6.	4 + 3 =	4 + 8 =	1 + 4 =	4 + 4 =
7.	9 + 4 =	4 + 5 =	7 + 4 =	4 + 7 =
8.	3 + 4 =	0 + 4 =	4 + 2 =	4 + 9 =
9.	4 + 1 =	6 + 4 =	4 + 6 =	2 + 4 =
10.	8 + 4 =	4 + 0 =	5 + 4 =	9 + 4 =

ADDITION — 4'S

EXERCISE 61. — THE COMBINATIONS

1. $\frac{1}{4}$ $\frac{2}{4}$ $\frac{3}{4}$ $\frac{4}{4}$ $\frac{5}{4}$ $\frac{6}{4}$ $\frac{7}{4}$ $\frac{8}{4}$ $\frac{9}{4}$ $\frac{0}{4}$

2. $\frac{4}{1}$ $\frac{4}{2}$ $\frac{4}{3}$ $\frac{4}{4}$ $\frac{4}{5}$ $\frac{4}{6}$ $\frac{4}{7}$ $\frac{4}{8}$ $\frac{4}{9}$ $\frac{4}{0}$

3. $\frac{4}{4}$ $\frac{7}{4}$ $\frac{3}{4}$ $\frac{6}{4}$ $\frac{8}{4}$ $\frac{1}{4}$ $\frac{9}{4}$ $\frac{0}{4}$ $\frac{2}{4}$ $\frac{5}{4}$

4. $\frac{4}{8}$ $\frac{4}{5}$ $\frac{4}{2}$ $\frac{4}{6}$ $\frac{4}{0}$ $\frac{4}{3}$ $\frac{4}{7}$ $\frac{4}{9}$ $\frac{4}{1}$ $\frac{4}{4}$

5. $\frac{5}{4}$ $\frac{4}{4}$ $\frac{2}{4}$ $\frac{4}{1}$ $\frac{0}{4}$ $\frac{4}{9}$ $\frac{9}{4}$ $\frac{4}{7}$ $\frac{1}{4}$ $\frac{4}{3}$

6. $\frac{8}{4}$ $\frac{4}{0}$ $\frac{6}{4}$ $\frac{4}{6}$ $\frac{3}{4}$ $\frac{4}{2}$ $\frac{7}{4}$ $\frac{4}{5}$ $\frac{4}{8}$ $\frac{4}{4}$

7. 4 and what other number will make each of these numbers: 9; 6; 4; 13; 5; 10; 12; 7; 11; 8?

ADDITION — 4'S

EXERCISE 62. — ORAL PROBLEMS

1. The big can holds 9 quarts. The little can holds 4 quarts. Both cans hold — quarts.

2. A man cuts a stick into 4 pieces. He cuts another stick into 5 pieces. He then has — pieces.

3. Jack paid 4 cents for some milk. He has 6 cents left. At first he had — cents.

4. Will has 4 marbles. Rob has 8 more marbles than Will. Rob has — marbles.

5. The little pole is 7 feet long. The big one is 4 feet longer. The big pole is — feet long.

6. How many legs has 1 horse? How many legs have 2 horses?

7. Ned is 4 years old. How old will he be 3 years from now?

8. There are 2 boys and 4 girls in the room. How many children are there in the room?

9. Ann's piece of paper is 8 inches long. May's piece is 4 inches longer. How long is May's?

ADDITION — 4'S

EXERCISE 63. — INCREASING NUMBERS OF TWO ORDERS

1.	1 __4__	11 __4__	21 __4__	41 __4__	61 __4__	80 __4__	30 __4__	50 __4__
2.	2 __4__	12 __4__	22 __4__	52 __4__	13 __4__	93 __4__	43 __4__	63 __4__
3.	4 __4__	14 __4__	23 __4__	74 __4__	94 __4__	44 __4__	64 __4__	84 __4__
4.	5 __4__	15 __4__	25 __4__	85 __4__	35 __4__	55 __4__	75 __4__	95 __4__
5.	6 __4__	16 __4__	26 __4__	96 __4__	46 __4__	66 __4__	86 __4__	36 __4__
6.	7 __4__	17 __4__	27 __4__	57 __4__	77 __4__	97 __4__	47 __4__	67 __4__
7.	8 __4__	18 __4__	28 __4__	68 __4__	88 __4__	38 __4__	58 __4__	78 __4__
8.	9 __4__	19 __4__	29 __4__	79 __4__	99 __4__	49 __4__	69 __4__	89 __4__

ADDITION — 4'S

EXERCISE 64. — COUNTING BY 4'S

1. Read the numbers in bold figures:

1,   2,   3,   **4,**   5,   6,   7,   **8,**
9,   10, 11, **12,** 13, 14, 15, **16,**
17, 18, 19, **20,** 21, 22, 23, **24,**
25, 26, 27, **28,** 29, 30, 31, **32,**
33, 34, 35, **36,** 37, 38, 39, **40**

2. Name the sums:

0 + 4,   4 + 4,   8 + 4,   12 + 4,   16 + 4,
20 + 4, 24 + 4, 28 + 4, 32 + 4,   36 + 4.

3. Count these dots by 4's:

4. Count by 4's:

4, 4, 4, 4, 4, 4, 4, 4, 4, 4.

5. Find the sum of the 4's in each box:

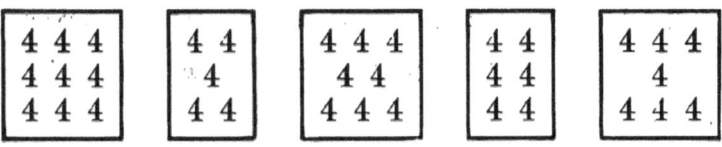

ADDITION — 4'S

EXERCISE 65. — PROBLEMS (COUNTING BY 4'S)

1. Here are — horses. Each horse has — legs. They all have — legs.

2. I see — dogs. Each dog has — legs. They all have — legs.

8. There are — cows in the lot. Each cow has — legs. They all have — legs.

4. The house has — windows. Each window has — panes of glass. The — windows have — panes of glass.

5. Jack has 4 boxes. In each box he places 4 marbles. He places — marbles in the boxes.

6. One pad costs 4 cents. How much will 8 pads cost?

SUBTRACTION — 4'S

EXERCISE 66. — DEVELOPMENT

4 + ? = 5
How many are 5 — 4?

1 + ? = 5
How many are 5 — 1?

4 + ? = 6
How many are 6 — 4?

2 + ? = 6
How many are 6 — 2?

4 + ? = 7
How many are 7 — 4?

3 + ? = 7
How many are 7 — 3?

4 + ? = 8
How many are 8 — 4?

4 + ? = 8
How many are 8 — 4?

4 + ? = 9
How many are 9 — 4?

5 + ? = 9
How many are 9 — 5?

4 + ? = 10
How many are 10 — 4?

6 + ? = 10
How many are 10 — 6?

4 + ? = 11
How many are 11 — 4?

7 + ? = 11
How many are 11 — 7?

4 + ? = 12
How many are 12 — 4?

8 + ? = 12
How many are 12 — 8?

4 + ? = 13
How many are 13 — 4?

9 + ? = 13
How many are 13 — 9?

SUBTRACTION — 4'S

EXERCISE 67. — THE COMBINATIONS

1. $\underline{6}\atop 4$ $\underline{7}\atop 4$ $\underline{8}\atop 4$ $\underline{9}\atop 4$ $\underline{10}\atop 4$ $\underline{11}\atop 4$ $\underline{12}\atop 4$ $\underline{13}\atop 4$

2. 6 7 8 9 10 11 12 13
    2 4 4 5   6   7   8   9

3. 7 9 12 8 11 6 13 10
    4 4   4 4   4 4   4   4

4. 10 5 13 9 12 7 11 8
     6 2   9 5   8 3   7 4

5. 13 8 11 10 4 12 9 4
     4 4   7   4 4   8 5 0

6. 6 11 9 10 5 5 12 13
    2   4 4   6 1 4   4   9

7. 8 - 4 =   10 - 6 =   9 - 4 =   11 - 7 =
8. 11 - 4 =   7 - 4 =   9 - 5 =   12 - 4 =
9. 13 - 9 =   10 - 4 =   13 - 4 =   12 - 8 =

SUBTRACTION — 4'S

EXERCISE 68. — ORAL PROBLEMS

1. Ann buys a dozen eggs. She uses 4 eggs. — eggs remain.

2. This string was 13 inches long. I cut off 4 inches. It is now — inches long.

8. There were a dozen chairs in the room. 8 of them were taken away. — chairs were left.

4. Jack buys a pencil and a pad for 10 cents. The pencil costs 4 cents. The pad costs — cents.

6. I pay 11 cents for two books. One of them costs 7 cents. The other costs — cents.

6. Rob has a dime. He buys a 6-cent pad. How much money has he left?

7. In a lot there are 9 trees. 4 of them are taken away. How many trees remain?

8. Rob has 13 marbles. Ned has 9 less than that. How many marbles has Ned?

9. In the first row there are 4 girls. In the second row there are 8 girls. Which row has the more girls? How many more?

SUBTRACTION — 4'S

EXERCISE 69. — DECREASING NUMBERS OF TWO ORDERS

1.
5	15	25	65	45	94	84	74
4	4	4	4	4	4	4	4

2.
6	16	26	46	17	37	57	77
4	4	4	4	4	4	4	4

3.
8	18	28	58	98	48	38	68
4	4	4	4	4	4	4	4

4.
59	19	29	89	79	69	49	39
4	4	4	4	4	4	4	4

5.
10	20	30	70	90	50	80	60
4	4	4	4	4	4	4	4

6.
11	21	31	51	71	41	81	61
4	4	4	4	4	4	4	4

7.
12	22	32	72	52	82	42	92
4	4	4	4	4	4	4	4

8.
13	23	33	63	93	43	73	53
4	4	4	4	4	4	4	4

ADDITION AND SUBTRACTION — 4'S

EXERCISE 70. — WRITTEN EXAMPLES

Add:

	(1)	(2)	(3)	(4)	(5)	(6)	(7)	(8)
	1	2	4	2	4	4	3	4
	2	1	1	4	3	4	2	4
	2	3	4	1	4	1	4	4
	3	4	2	4	3	3	4	4
A.	4	4	4	3	4	4	3	4

	(1)	(2)	(3)	(4)	(5)	(6)	(7)	(8)
	32	23	34	21	44	32	13	42
	12	30	40	40	10	34	34	14
	20	14	14	14	20	10	41	21
B.	34	22	11	12	11	12	10	10

	(1)	(2)	(3)	(4)	(5)	(6)	(7)	(8)
	12	22	31	20	22	14	20	11
	34	12	20	13	44	13	20	42
	11	24	4	41	12	40	8	14
	21	10	12	12	10	10	10	20
C.	20	21	20	13	11	21	30	11

Subtract:

	(1)	(2)	(3)	(4)	(5)	(6)	(7)	(8)
	99	87	62	70	49	38	57	89
D.	34	44	22	30	44	14	15	64

	(1)	(2)	(3)	(4)	(5)	(6)	(7)	(8)
	69	85	28	47	94	83	78	99
E.	23	41	24	14	42	41	34	45

OBJECTIVE SOLUTIONS

EXERCISE 71. — PROBLEMS

1. Here are 6 marbles. Place them in boxes. Place 2 marbles in each box. How many boxes do you need?

2. A pencil costs 3 cents. How many pencils can you buy for 18 cents?

3. How many 4-cent pads can you buy with 20 cents?

4. I place 16 apples on plates. On each plate I place 4 apples. How many plates do I need?

6. Here is a string 12 inches long. Cut it into pieces 3 inches long. How many pieces are there?

6. A man plants 15 trees in rows. He plants 3 trees in each row. How many rows does he plant?

7. A milkman has 12 pints of milk. He puts the milk into cans. Each can holds 2 pints. How many cans does he use?

NOTE. Problems of this division type (measuring) are easily solved by grouping objects and counting. For example, the pupil solves Ko. 1 by taking 6 splints, placing them in groups of two and counting the groups.

OBJECTIVE SOLUTIONS

EXERCISE 72. — PROBLEMS

1. Here are 3 boxes and 12 marbles. Place the same number of marbles in each box. How many marbles are there in each box?

2. In 4 nests there are 20 eggs. Each nest has the same number of eggs. How many eggs are there in each nest?

3. There are 18 trees in rows. There are 3 rows. How many trees are there in each row?

4. A man gives 16 cents to 4 boys. He gives the same number of cents to each boy. How much does he give to each boy?

5. I give 12 marbles to 2 boys. I give the same number of marbles to each boy. How many do I give to each boy?

6. Five pads cost 15 cents. They all cost the same. How much does one pad cost?

Note. Problems of this division type (partition) are easily solved by grouping objects and counting. For example, the pupil solves No. 1 by taking 12 splints, distributing them one at a time in rotation among three groups and counting the splints in a group.

ADDITION AND SUBTRACTION

EXERCISE 73. — WRITTEN PROBLEMS

(1)
Jack, 36 years old.
Father, 42 years older.
Father, — years old.

(2)
Mother, 48 years old.
Kate, 22 years younger.
Kate, — years old.

3. Mr. May buys 14 sheep, 32 sheep, 43 sheep, and 10 sheep. How many sheep does he buy?

4. Ann plants 11 seeds, 34 seeds, 20 seeds, and 22 seeds. How many seeds does she plant?

6. Rob has a rope 43 feet long, Ned has a rope 26 feet longer. How long is Ned's rope?

6. A house is 35 feet high. A tree is 89 feet high. How much higher is the tree?

7. One can holds 48 quarts. Another can holds 13 quarts. How many more quarts does the first can hold than the second?

8. Ned's father is 69 years old. Rob's father is 63 years old. Which is older? How much?

9. In three rooms there are 32, 40, and 34 boys. There are — boys in the rooms.

ADDITION AND SUBTRACTION

10. A table costs $67. A chair costs $24. Which costs more? How much more?

U. In a school there are 97 boys. One day 25 of them were absent. How many were present?

12. I paid $53 for a wagon. I paid $34 more than that for a horse. How much did I pay for the horse?

13. Jack cut a pole into four pieces. Each piece was 12 feet long. How long was the pole?

14. A man plants 21, 30, 17, and 20 trees. How many trees does he plant?

16. Ned cut a pole into three pieces. The pieces were 13, 25, and 40 feet long. How long was the pole?

16. A man had 76 quarts of milk. He sold 42 quarts. How much did he have left?

17. I wish to buy a table. The table costs $45. I have $30. How much more money do I need?

18. Ned is 13 years old. In how many more years will he be 39 years old?

ADDITION — 2'S, 3'S AND 4'S

EXERCISE 74. — MISCELLANEOUS COMBINATIONS

1.   4   5   7   9   2   1   6   0   4   3
     8   4   3   2   3   4   2   4   3   2

2.   2   3   5   3   5   3   4   6   1   7
     2   9   2   4   3   0   4   3   2   2

3.   2   3   6   3   8   1   4   9   3   4
     4   8   4   7   2   3   7   3   3   2

4.   4   3   8   0   7   2   9   8   3   2
     5   6   3   3   4   5   4   4   5   7

5.   9   2   4   2   4   8   0   4   2   3
     4   6   0   8   9   3   2   6   9   9

6.   6 + 2 =   5 + 4 =   4 + 9 =   4 + 2 =

7.   4 + 0 =   6 + 3 =   2 + 2 =   8 + 3 =

8.   3 + 8 =   8 + 2 =   9 + 4 =   4 + 0 =

9.   4 + 6 =   9 + 3 =   8 + 4 =   4 + 5 =

10. 2 + 5 =   7 + 3 =   4 + 7 =   3 + 8 =

SUBTRACTION — 2'S, 3'S AND 4'S

EXERCISE 75. — MISCELLANEOUS COMBINATIONS

1.   9   7   6   9   10   8   11   10
    4   3   2   3   2   6   7   3

2.   6   8   7   11   9   8   13   12
    3   4   4   3   2   5   4   8

3.   5   3   7   9   13   8   11   10
    2   3   2   6   9   3   9   7

4.   9   6   8   10   7   10   5   11
    7   4   2   6   5   8   4   4

5.   9   5   12   12   11   11   10   12
    5   3   9   4   2   8   4   3

6.   13 - 9 =   10 - 6 =   12 - 9 =   11 - 2 =

7.   12 - 4 =   11 - 3 =   10 - 7 =   13 - 4 =

8.   11 - 7 =   10 - 2 =   12 - 3 =   11 - 4 =

9.   11 - 8 =   12 - 8 =   11 - 9 =   10 - 3 =

10.   9 - 5 =   8 - 2 =   7 - 4 =   8 - 5 =

ADDITION — 2'S, 3'S AND 4'S

EXERCISE 76. — INCREASING NUMBERS OF TWO ORDERS

	18	33	48	25	60	38	57	79
1.	4	2	3	4	3	2	4	2

	55	89	66	74	41	13	26	77
2.	3	4	4	3	2	4	3	2

	63	52	47	69	44	85	70	36
3.	3	4	2	3	4	2	4	4

	85	56	78	92	16	30	64	23
4.	2	3	4	2	4	3	2	4

	46	70	59	31	22	88	17	82
5.	2	3	4	3	4	2	3	4

	37	65	81	45	76	91	29	12
6.	4	3	2	2	4	4	3	2

	99	10	51	86	53	42	24	39
7.	1	4	3	2	2	3	3	2

	73	27	83	40	65	32	58	97
8.	2	4	4	2	2	4	3	3

SUBTRACTION — 2'S, 3'S AND 4'S

EXERCISE 77. — DECREASING NUMBERS OF TWO ORDERS

1. 87 54 96 73 50 27 91 75
     3   2   3   2   4   4   4   3

2. 68 40 93 10 37 46 65 51
     3   3   4   4   4   2   3   3

3. 85 70 81 86 43 32 49 63
     2   3   2   2   4   3   3   3

4. 45 53 84 58 78 55 52 78
     2   4   3   3   2   3   4   4

5. 42 63 97 17 18 89 47 92
     3   2   3   4   4   3   2   2

6. 24 35 19 59 33 66 69 50
     3   4   2   3   4   3   4   2

7. 39 54 86 48 74 44 30 17
     2   4   3   3   4   2   3   3

8. 18 25 41 85 64 82 58 95
     4   3   2   3   3   4   2   3

EXERCISE 78. — WRITING NUMBERS

Write these numbers:

1. Fifty-six; thirty-four; seventy-three; twelve.
2. Forty-one; sixty-seven; eighty-eight; eleven.
3. Ninety-five; twenty-nine; thirty; seventeen.
4. Twenty-three; fifty-five; fifteen; seventy.
5. Eighty-four; ninety-eight; thirty-two; ten.
6. Thirty-eight; forty-six; sixty-nine; ninety.
7. Sixty-six; eighty-seven; seventy-one; fifty.
8. Seventy-five; forty-four; fifty-three; twenty.
9. Twenty-eight; forty-nine; fourteen; sixty-four.
10. Eighty-two; ninety-three; thirty-three; sixteen.
11. Thirteen; forty-seven; twenty-six; ninety-nine.
12. Ninety-six; fifty-eight; sixty-five; eighteen.
13. Forty-eight; eighty-one; ninety-four; sixty.
14. Fifty-nine; thirty-seven; twenty-two; forty.
15. Thirty-five; seventy-six; eighty; eighty-nine.

PART III
NUMBERS THROUGH 999

EXERCISE 79. — READING

1.	496	832	648	796	837	305	600
2.	316	745	983	765	216	310	805
3.	505	189	990	467	220	450	500
4.	698	111	555	628	967	554	339
5.	127	980	747	353	888	475	959
6.	533	479	795	225	689	763	542
7.	426	837	656	489	748	785	952
8.	989	878	358	767	545	434	323

NOTATION AND NUMERATION

EXERCISE 80. — ROMAN NUMERALS THROUGH XII

Another way of writing the numbers from 1 to 12 is:

I = 1	V = 5	IX = 9
II = 2	VI = 6	X = 10
III = 3	VII = 7	XI = 11
IV = 4	VIII = 8	XII = 12

These new numbers are called Roman numbers.

1. Name each of these Roman numbers, and write them in another way:

X, I, VI, II, IX, III, VIII, IV, V, XII, VII, XI.

2. Write each of these numbers in the Roman way: 9, 12, 8, 1, 5, 10, 2, 7, 4, 6, 11, 3.

NOTE. On most clock faces *four* is written IIII.

ADDITION—5'S

EXERCISE 81. — THE COMBINATIONS WITH OBJECTS

ADDITION—5'S

EXERCISE 82. — TABLE

1 + 5 =	6 + 5 =	5 + 1 =	5 + 6 =
2 + 5 =	7 + 5 =	5 + 2 =	5 + 7 =
3 + 5 =	8 + 5 =	5 + 3 =	5 + 8 =
4 + 5 =	9 + 5 =	5 + 4 =	5 + 9 =
5 + 5 =	0 + 5 =	5 + 5 =	5 + 0 =

1. 5 balls and 9 balls are — balls.
2. 7 houses and 5 houses are — houses.
3. 5 years and 5 years are — years.
4. 8 girls and 5 girls are — girls.
5. 5 plates and 6 plates are — plates.

6. 2 + 5 =	5 + 1 =	9 + 5 =	5 + 9 =
7. 6 + 5 =	5 + 3 =	5 + 2 =	1 + 5 =
8. 5 + 7 =	0 + 5 =	4 + 5 =	5 + 0 =
9. 3 + 5 =	5 + 4=	8 + 5 =	5 + 6 =
10. 5 + 9 =	5 + 5 =	7 + 5 =	5 + 8 =

ADDITION—5'S

EXERCISE 83. — THE COMBINATIONS

1. $\frac{1}{5}$ $\frac{2}{5}$ $\frac{3}{5}$ $\frac{4}{5}$ $\frac{5}{5}$ $\frac{6}{5}$ $\frac{7}{5}$ $\frac{8}{5}$ $\frac{9}{5}$ $\frac{0}{5}$

2. $\frac{5}{1}$ $\frac{5}{2}$ $\frac{5}{3}$ $\frac{5}{4}$ $\frac{5}{5}$ $\frac{5}{6}$ $\frac{5}{7}$ $\frac{5}{8}$ $\frac{5}{9}$ $\frac{5}{0}$

3. $\frac{6}{5}$ $\frac{0}{5}$ $\frac{8}{5}$ $\frac{5}{5}$ $\frac{3}{5}$ $\frac{9}{5}$ $\frac{7}{5}$ $\frac{1}{5}$ $\frac{4}{5}$ $\frac{2}{5}$

4. $\frac{5}{3}$ $\frac{5}{7}$ $\frac{5}{4}$ $\frac{5}{2}$ $\frac{5}{1}$ $\frac{5}{6}$ $\frac{5}{5}$ $\frac{5}{9}$ $\frac{5}{0}$ $\frac{5}{8}$

5. $\frac{2}{5}$ $\frac{5}{9}$ $\frac{1}{5}$ $\frac{5}{8}$ $\frac{4}{5}$ $\frac{5}{0}$ $\frac{3}{5}$ $\frac{5}{6}$ $\frac{7}{5}$ $\frac{5}{5}$

6. $\frac{9}{5}$ $\frac{5}{1}$ $\frac{6}{5}$ $\frac{5}{3}$ $\frac{0}{5}$ $\frac{5}{7}$ $\frac{8}{5}$ $\frac{5}{4}$ $\frac{5}{9}$ $\frac{5}{2}$

7. 5 and what other number will make each of these numbers: 14; 10; 8; 5; 13; 9; 12; 7; 11; 6?

ADDITION—5'S

EXERCISE 84. — ORAL PROBLEMS

1. There are 9 balls on the table. I place 5 more there. — balls are now on the table.

2. Will brings some roses to school. He gives 6 to May and Kate. He has 5 left. He brings — roses.

3. On one hand there are — fingers. On both hands there are — fingers.

4. In one nest there are 7 eggs. In another nest there are 5 eggs. In both nests there are — eggs.

5. The red pole is 8 feet long. The black pole is 5 feet longer. The black pole is — feet long.

6. Ned buys some milk for 5 cents. He has 9 cents left. How much did he have at first?

7. There are 5 apples on a plate. I place 4 apples more on the plate. How many apples are now on the plate?

8. May has 5 cents. Ann has 6 cents more than May. How many cents has Ann?

ADDITION—5'S

EXERCISE 85. — INREASING NUMBERS OF TWO ORDERS

1.	1 5	11 5	21 5	41 5	61 5	80 5	90 5	30 5
2.	2 5	12 5	22 5	62 5	13 5	93 5	33 5	33 5
3.	4 5	14 5	24 5	94 5	34 5	54 5	74 5	44 5
4.	5 5	15 5	25 5	35 5	55 5	75 5	45 5	65 5
5.	6 5	16 5	26 5	56 5	76 5	46 5	66 5	86 5
6.	7 5	17 5	27 5	77 5	47 5	67 5	87 5	97 5
7.	8 5	18 5	28 5	48 5	68 5	88 5	98 5	38 5
8.	9 5	19 5	29 5	69 5	89 5	99 5	39 5	59 5

ADDITION—5'S

EXERCISE 86. — COUNTING BY 5'S

1. Read the numbers in bold figures:

```
 1   12   23   34   45    7   18   29   40
11   22   33   44    6   17   28   39   50
21   32   43    5   16   27   38   49
31   42    4   15   26   37   48   10
41    3   14   25   36   47    9   20
 2   13   24   35   46    8   19   30
```

2. Name the sums:

0 + 5,   5 + 5,   10 + 5,   15 + 5,   20 + 5,
25 + 5, 30 + 5, 35 + 5,   40 + 5,   45 + 5.

3. Count these dots by 5's:

4. Count by 5's:

5, 5, 5, 5, 5, 5, 5, 5, 5, 5.

6. Find the sum of the 5's in each box:

```
┌─────────┐  ┌──────┐  ┌─────────┐  ┌──────┐  ┌─────────┐
│ 5  5  5 │  │ 5  5 │  │ 5  5  5 │  │ 5  5 │  │ 5  5  5 │
│ 5  5  5 │  │ 5  5 │  │    5    │  │   5  │  │   5  5  │
│ 5  5  5 │  │ 5  5 │  │ 5  5  5 │  │ 5  5 │  │ 5  5  5 │
└─────────┘  └──────┘  └─────────┘  └──────┘  └─────────┘
```

ADDITION—5'S

EXERCISE 87. — PROBLEMS (COUNTING BY 5'S)

1. 🍌 🍌 🍌 🍌 🍌 Here are — bananas. At 3 for 5¢ they cost — cents.

2. o o o o o o o o These are — nickels. For these nickels I can get — cents in change.

3. ☕ ☕ ☕ ☕ ☕ At 5¢ each, these cups cost — cents.

4. ••• ••• Two apples cost 5¢. Six apples cost — cents.

5. How many fingers are there on one hand? How many fingers are there on eight hands?

OBJECTIVE SOLUTIONS

EXERCISE 88. — WRITTEN PROBLEMS

1. I buy some pencils for 18 cents. Each pencil costs 3 cents. How many pencils do I buy?

2. I give 24 apples to some boys. I give each boy 4 apples. How many boys receive apples?

3. I pour 16 pints of milk into some cans. I pour 2 pints into each can. How many cans do I need?

4. Mr. May plants 25 seeds in boxes. He plants 5 seeds in each box. How many boxes does he use?

5. Here is a strip of paper 36 inches long. Cut it into pieces 4 inches long. How many pieces are there?

6. Jack cuts a stick 50 feet long into pieces. Each piece is 5 feet long. How many pieces are there?

7. How many 3-cent pads can I buy for 24 cents?

NOTE. As to method of solution, gee footnote, p. 86.

OBJECTIVE SOLUTIONS

EXERCISE 89. — WRITTEN PROBLEMS

1. Mr. May puts 12 quarts of milk into 2 cans. Each can receives the same amount How much does he put into each can?

2. Put 20 cents into 5 boxes. Let there be the same amount in each box. How many cents are there in each box?

3. I give 18 jacks to Ann, May, and Rose. Each girl receives the same number. How many does each girl receive?

4. Five coats of the same kind cost $35. How much does one coat cost?

5. Three girls together have 27 jacks. Each has the same number. How many has each?

6. There are 36 sheep in 4 lots. In each lot there is the same number. How many sheep are there in each lot?

7. You may put 18 marbles into 3 boxes. Into each box put the same number. How many marbles are there in each box?

NOTE. As to method of solution, see footnote, p. 87.

SUBTRACTION—5'S

EXERCISE 90. — DEVELOPMENT

5 + ? = 6	1 + ? = 6
How many are 6 - 5?	How many are 6 - 1?
5 + ? = 7	2 + ? = 7
How many are 7 - 5?	How many are 7 - 2?
5 + ? = 8	3 + ? = 8
How many are 8 - 5?	How many are 8 - 3?
5 + ? = 9	4 + ? = 9
How many are 9 - 5?	How many are 9 - 4?
5 + ? = 10	5 + ? = 10
How many are 10 - 5?	How many are 10 - 5?
5 + ? = 11	6 + ? = 11
How many are 11 - 5?	How many are 11 - 6?
5 + ? = 12	7 + ? = 12
How many are 12 - 5?	How many are 12 - 7?
5 + ? = 13	8 + ? = 13
How many are 13 - 5?	How many are 13 - 8?
5 + ? = 14	9 + ? = 14
How many are 14 - 5?	How many are 14 - 9?

SUBTRACTION—5'S

EXERCISE 91. — THE COMBINATIONS

1.   7   8   9   10   11   12   13   14
        5   5   5   5   5   5   5   5

2.   7   8   9   10   11   12   13   14
        2   3   4   5   6   7   8   9

3.   9   6   8   14   12   10   13   11
        5   5   5   5   5   5   5   5

4.   8   5   9   6   13   14   11   12
        3   0   4   1   8   9   6   7

5.   14   10   8   12   7   11   14   13
        9   5   3   7   5   6   5   8

6.   12   8   13   11   9   9   6   14
        5   5   5   5   4   5   5   9

7.   14-5=   11-5=   13-5=   10-5 =

8.   12-5=   13-8=   12-7=   11-6 =

9.   7-5=   14-9=   9-5=   8-5 =

SUBTRACTION—5'S

EXERCISE 92. — ORAL PROBLEMS

1. Rob has a dime. He buys a pint of milk for 5 cents. He has — cents left.

2. Ann wants to buy a 14-cent book. She has only 5 cents. She needs — cents more.

3. There were 8 apples on the table. 5 of them were not good. — apples were good.

4. A stick is 1 foot long. It is — inches long. Ned cuts off 5 inches. — inches are left.

5. Ann has a dozen roses. She gives 5 of them to May. She has — roses left.

6. May is 5 years old. In how many years will she be 11 years old?

7. Jack buys 13 roses. Ann buys 5 roses. Jack buys — more roses than Ann.

8. In a box there were 9 eggs. A boy took 5 of them. How many eggs were left?

9. Ned buys a 6¢ book. He pays 5¢ less for a pencil. How much does the pencil cost?

SUBTRACTION—5'S

EXERCISE 93. — DECREASING NUMBERS OF TWO ORDERS

	6	16	26	56	86	65	95	45
1.	5	5	5	5	5	5	5	5

	7	17	27	87	18	98	48	38
2.	5	5	5	5	5	5	5	5

	9	19	29	99	49	39	79	59
3.	5	5	5	5	5	5	5	5

	10	20	30	40	70	50	80	60
4.	5	5	5	5	5	5	5	5

	11	21	14	31	71	51	81	61
5.	5	5	5	5	5	5	5	5

	12	22	32	72	52	82	65	92
6.	5	5	5	5	5	5	5	5

	13	23	73	53	83	63	93	43
7.	5	5	5	5	5	5	5	5

	14	24	54	84	64	94	44	34
8.	5	5	5	5	5	5	5	5

SUBTRACTION—5'S

EXERCISE 94. — WRITTEN EXAMPLES

Add:

	(1)	(2)	(3)	(4)	(5)	(6)	(7)
	5	5	5	5	5	5	5
	3	1	4	4	4	5	4
	4	4	4	5	2	5	5
	2	2	3	3	5	5	5
A.	3	5	3	5	5	5	5

	(1)	(2)	(3)	(4)	(5)	(6)	(7)
	25	35	40	43	45	54	34
	30	54	51	15	25	45	25
	55	45	34	50	32	53	43
B.	54	50	55	24	15	55	52

	(1)	(2)	(3)	(4)	(5)	(6)	(7)
	123	412	332	25	53	314	214
	204	115	120	230	604	25	33
	345	305	241	53	45	32	75
	12	33	110	540	22	545	404
C	111	102	155	51	103	35	123

Subtract:

	(1)	(2)	(3)	(4)	(5)	(6)	(7)
	558	938	745	990	878	476	650
D.	503	535	520	450	523	351	550

	(1)	(2)	(3)	(4)	(5)	(6)	(7)
	786	459	953	382	599	258	776
E.	535	54	503	30	455	155	256

FRACTIONS

EXERCISE 95. — HALVES AND FOURTHS

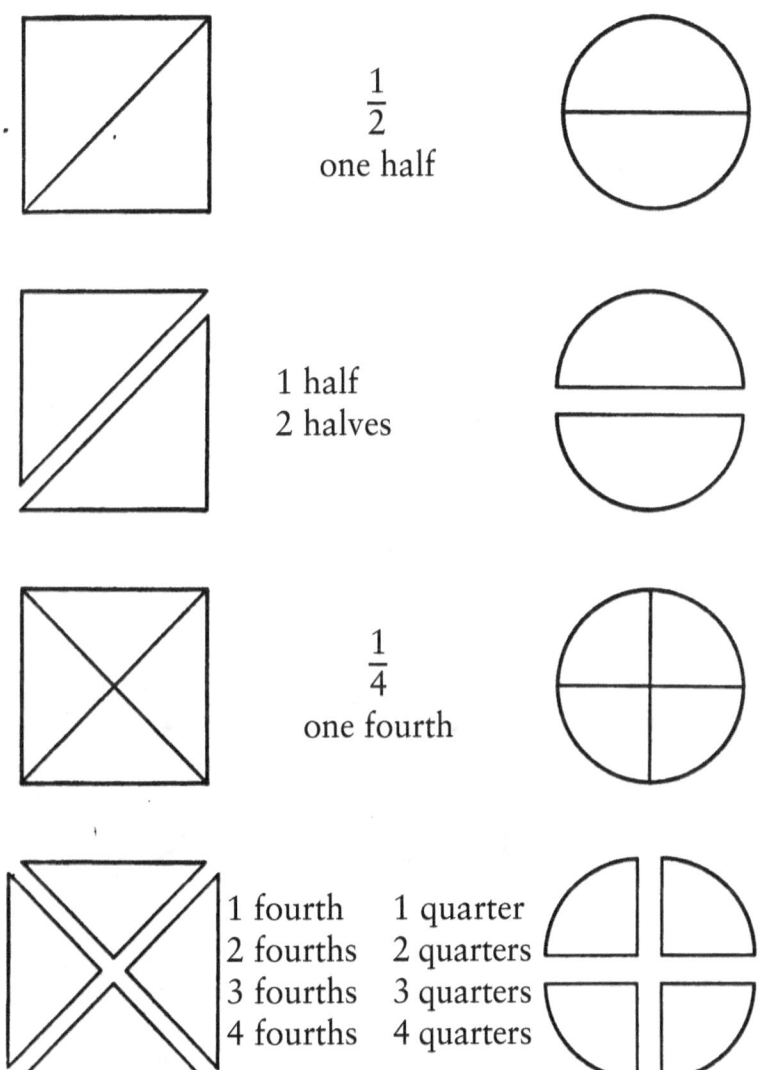

MEASUREMENTS

EXERCISE 96. — TIME: HOUR, HALF-HOUR, QUARTER-HOUR

What time does each clock show?

EXERCISE 97. — PASTS OF A DOLLAR

In one dollar there are — half dollars.

In one dollar there are — quarter dollars.

In one dollar there are — dimes.

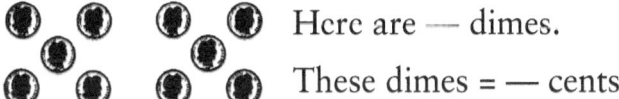 Here are — dimes.
These dimes = — cents.

In one dollar there are — cents.

In one half dollar there are — cents.

In one half dollar there are — quarters.

 Here are — nickels.
These nickels = — cents.

In one half dollar there are — cents.

In one quarter dollar there are — cents.

MAKING CHANGE

EXERCISE 98. — BUYING AND SELLING

1. I buy some apples for 17¢. I pay for them with a half dollar. Please make the change.

2. A boy buys meat that costs 36 cents. He pays for it with a half dollar. Make the change.

3. Here is a quarter. Please change it for nickels.

4. I give a half dollar to pay for a ride on the car. Please give me the change.

5. Here is a dollar. Please change it so that I shall receive four nickels.

6. I have a quarter with which I pay for some bread that costs 9 cents. Let me have the change.

7. May buys milk for 8 cents. She pays with a quarter. Make the change.

8. Ned buys a 2¢ pencil and a 4¢ pad. He pays.with a dime. Make the change.

9. I give a half dollar to pay for some meat. The meat costs 27 cents. Make the change.

MAKING CHANGE

10. Give me change in 2 quarters and in dimes for a dollar.

11. I pay for a 43-cent book with a dollar. Make the change.

12. I pay for a 73-cent book with a dollar. Make the change.

13. May buys meat that costs 87 cents. She pays for it with a dollar. Make the change.

14. I give you a quarter to pay for a ride on the car. Give me the change.

16. Some apples cost me 45 cents. I pay for them with a dollar. Give me the change.

16. I have 32 cents. I wish to pay for a 50-cent book. Please give me the money I need.

17. I have 58 cents. I wish to pay for a dollar book. Please let me have the money I need.

NOTE. Pupils should use toy or real money. As to method of making change, see footnote, p. 69. Problem 1, for example, is to be solved as follows: Pupil takes the half dollar, he names the price, 17 f, then gives in change 1¢, 1¢, 1¢, 5¢, and 25¢, saying, "18¢, 19¢, 20¢, 25¢, 50¢."

FRACTIONS

EXERCISE 99. — THIRDS AND SIXTHS

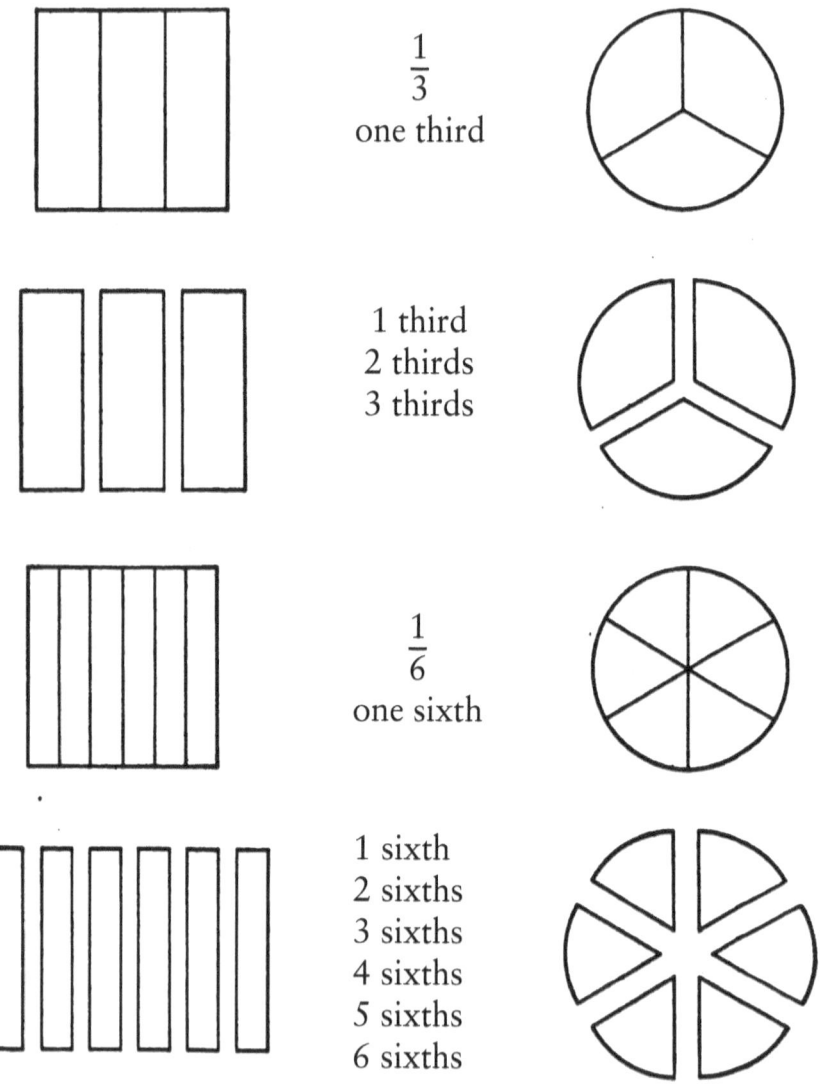

FRACTIONS

EXERCISE 100. — NAMING PARTS

How much of each figure is white?

How much of each figure is dark?

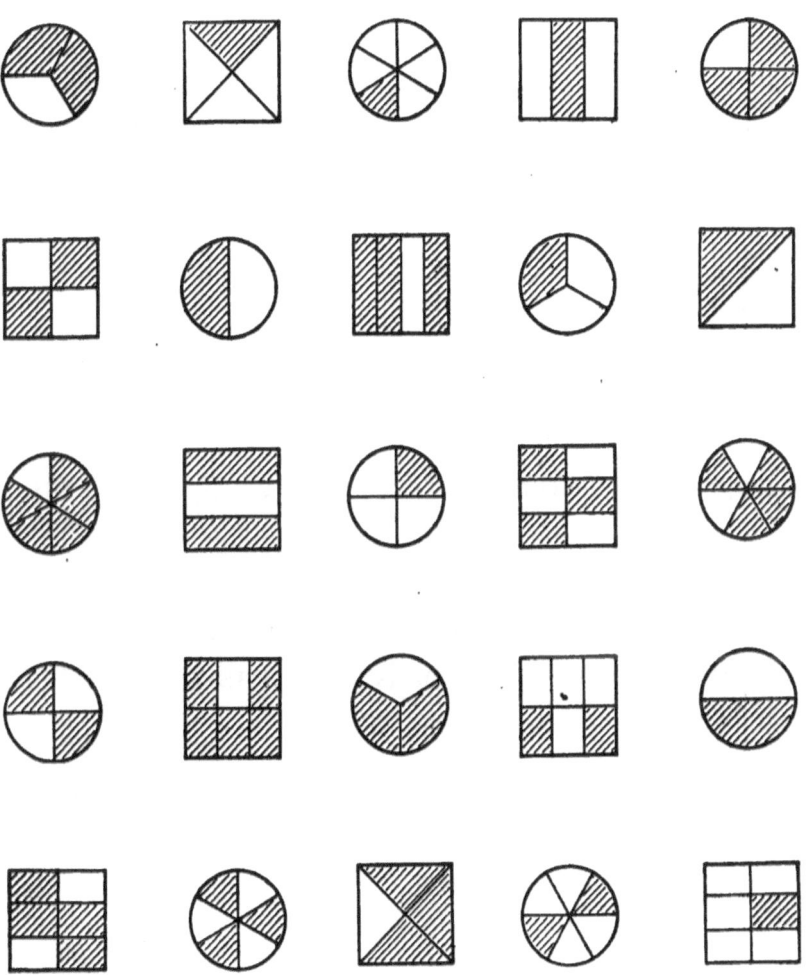

FRACTIONS

EXERCISE 101. — PROBLEMS

 1. Here are — pins. 1 half of 4 pins is — pins.

 2. Here are — pins. 1 third of 6 pins is — pins. 2 thirds of 6 pins are — pins.

 3. Jack has — marbles. -Jof 6 marbles is — marbles.

 4. May has — cents. 1 fourth of 8 cents is — cents. 3 fourths of 8 cents are — cents.

 5. Here are — balls. ⅓ of 9 balls is — balls, ⅔ of 9 balls are — balls.

 6. Here are — marbles. 1 sixth of 12 marbles is — marbles. 5 sixths of 12 marbles are — marbles.

ADDITION—6'S

EXERCISE 102. — COMBINATIONS WITH OBJECTS

ADDITION—6'S

EXERCISE 103. — TABLE

1 + 6 =	6 + 6 =	6 + 1 =	6 + 6 =
2 + 6 =	7 + 6 =	6 + 2 =	6 + 7 =
3 + 6 =	8 + 6 =	6 + 3 =	6 + 8 =
4 + 6 =	9 + 6 =	6 + 4 =	6 + 9 =
5 + 6 =	0 + 6 =	6 + 5 =	6 + 0 =

1. 6 pinks and 9 roses are — flowers.
2. 6 seeds and 6 seeds are — seeds.
3. 6 seats and 8 seats are — seats.
4. 7 inches and 6 inches are — inches.
5. 5 dollars and 6 dollars are — dollars.

6.	6 + 7 =	1 + 6 =	3 + 6 =	6 + 8 =
7.	6 + 6 =	6 + 2 =	4 + 6 =	6 + 9 =
8.	9 + 6 =	0 + 6 =	6 + 3 =	5 + 6 =
9.	5 + 6 =	6 + 1 =	6 + 4 =	7 + 6 =
10.	6 + 0 =	2 + 6 =	8 + 6 =	6 + 5 =

ADDITION—6'S

EXERCISE 104. — THE COMBINATIONS

	1	2	3	4	5	6	7	8	9	0
1.	6	6	6	6	6	6	6	6	6	6

	6	6	6	6	6	6	6	6	6	6
2.	1	2	3	4	5	6	7	8	9	0

	9	6	3	0	8	5	2	7	4	1
3.	6	6	6	6	6	6	6	6	6	6

	6	6	6	6	6	6	6	6	6	6
4.	3	5	7	9	0	4	8	2	6	1

	8	6	5	6	9	6	6	6	3	6
5.	1	0	6	4	6	3	6	9	6	7

	6	2	6	7	0	5	6	4	6	1
6.	5	6	1	6	6	6	2	6	8	6

7. 6 and what other number will make each of these numbers: 12; 7; 14; 8; 6; 10; 13; 15; 9; 11?

ADDITION—6'S

EXERCISE 105. — ORAL PROBLEMS

(1)
Eggs on plate,	6
Eggs in box,	9
Eggs in all,	?

(2)
Boys,	6
Girls,	7
Children,	?

(3)
Sheep in lot,	8
Sheep not in lot,	6
Sheep in all,	?

(4)
Pinks,	6
Roses,	6
Flowers,	?

5. Rose plants 7 seeds. May plants 6 seeds. How many seeds do the girls plant?

6. Jack draws a line 6 inches long. Ned draws a line 4 inches longer. How long is Ned's line?

7. In one row there are 6 seats. In another row there are 8 seats. How many seats are there in both rows?

8. Ned spends $6. He has $5 left. How much did he have at first?

9. I buy a coat for $9. I sell it so as to gain $6. For how much do I sell it?

10. A fly has 6 legs. How many legs have 2 flies?

ADDITION—6'S

EXERCISE 106. — INCREASING NUMBERS OF TWO ORDERS

1. | 1 | 11 | 21 | 51 | 81 | 30 | 70 | 90 |
    | 6 | 6 | 6 | 6 | 6 | 6 | 6 | 6 |

2. | 2 | 12 | 22 | 82 | 13 | 73 | 93 | 43 |
    | 6 | 6 | 6 | 6 | 6 | 6 | 6 | 6 |

3. | 4 | 14 | 24 | 74 | 94 | 44 | 64 | 54 |
    | 6 | 6 | 6 | 6 | 6 | 6 | 6 | 6 |

4. | 5 | 15 | 25 | 95 | 45 | 65 | 55 | 85 |
    | 6 | 6 | 6 | 6 | 6 | 6 | 6 | 6 |

5. | 6 | 16 | 26 | 46 | 66 | 56 | 86 | 36 |
    | 6 | 6 | 6 | 6 | 6 | 6 | 6 | 6 |

6. | 7 | 17 | 27 | 67 | 57 | 87 | 37 | 77 |
    | 6 | 6 | 6 | 6 | 6 | 6 | 6 | 6 |

7. | 8 | 18 | 28 | 58 | 88 | 38 | 78 | 98 |
    | 6 | 6 | 6 | 6 | 6 | 6 | 6 | 6 |

8. | 9 | 19 | 29 | 89 | 39 | 79 | 99 | 49 |
    | 6 | 6 | 6 | 6 | 6 | 6 | 6 | 6 |

ADDITION—6'S

EXERCISE 107. — PROBLEMS (ADDING BY 6'S)

1. In this picture there are — rows of men. In each row there are — men. In all the rows there are — men.

2. In each row there are — guns. In the first three rows there are — guns.

3. In the last two rows there are — guns.

4. 🥫 🥫 🥫 🥫 🥫 Into each of these cans I pour 6 pints of water. I use — pints of water.

5. 🍽 🍽 🍽 At 6¢ each, how much must I pay for these plates?

6. If one loaf of bread costs 6¢, what will be the cost of 6 loaves?

7. A fly has 6 legs. How many legs have 4 flies?

SUBTRACTION—6'S

EXERCISE 108. — DEVELOPMENT

6 + ? = 7
How many are 7 - 6?

1 + ? = 7
How many are 7 - 1?

6 + ? = 8
How many are 8 - 6?

2 + ? = 8
How many are 8 - 2?

6 + ? = 9
How many are 9 - 6?

3 + ? = 9
How many are 9 - 3?

6 + ? = 10
How many are 10 - 6?

4 + ? = 10
How many are 10 - 4?

6 + ? = 11
How many are 11 - 6?

5 + ? = 11
How many are 11 - 5?

6 + ? = 12
How many are 12 - 6?

6 + ? = 12
How many are 12 - 6?

6 + ? = 13
How many are 13 - 6?

7 + ? = 13
How many are 13 - 7?

6 + ? = 14
How many are 14 - 6?

8 + ? = 14
How many are 14 - 8?

6 + ? = 15
How many are 15 - 6?

9 + ? = 15
How many are 15 - 9?

SUBTRACTION—6'S

EXERCISE 109. — THE COMBINATIONS

1.   8/6   9/6   10/6   11/6   12/6   13/6   14/6   15/6

2.   8/2   9/3   10/4   11/5   12/6   13/7   14/8   15/9

3.   11/6   15/6   10/6   13/6   6/6   12/6   9/6   14/6

4.   14/8   9/3   11/5   15/9   10/4   13/7   7/1   6/0

5.   8/2   7/6   13/7   11/6   9/3   15/6   14/8   10/6

6.   11/5   15/9   13/6   10/4   9/6   8/6   14/6   12/6

7.   12 - 6 =   15 - 9 =   11 - 5 =   13 - 7 =

8.   15 - 6 =   14 - 8 =   13 - 6 =   10 - 4 =

9.   11 - 6 =   9 - 3 =   10 - 6 =   14 - 6 =

SUBTRACTION—6'S

EXERCISE 110. — ORAL PROBLEMS

	(1)			(2)	
	Pigs in all,	15		Apples in all,	13
	Pigs sold,	6		Apples good,	6
	Pigs not sold,	?		Apples not good,	?

	(3)			(4)	
	Bread and milk,	12¢		Boys and girls,	14
	Bread,	6¢		Boys,	6
	Milk,	?		Girls,	?

5. There are 11 trees on our block. On the next block there are 6 trees less. How many trees are there on the next block?

6. Jack draws a line 10 inches long. Ned draws a line 6 inches shorter. How long is Ned's line?

7. A farmer has 15 fruit trees. 6 are pear trees. The others are apple trees. How many apple trees has he?

8. A man buys a table for $9. He sells it at a loss of $6. For how much does he sell it?

9. Will left home at 6 o'clock. He came back at 12 o'clock. How long was he away?

SUBTRACTION—6'S

EXERCISE 111. — DECREASING NUMBERS OF TWO ORDERS

1.	7	17	27	47	87	56	36	76
	6	6	6	6	6	6	6	6

2.	8	18	28	88	19	39	79	99
	6	6	6	6	6	6	6	6

3.	10	20	50	30	70	90	60	40
	6	6	6	6	6	6	6	6

4.	11	21	31	71	91	61	41	81
	6	6	6	6	6	6	6	6

5.	12	22	72	92	62	42	82	52
	6	6	6	6	6	6	6	6

6.	13	23	93	63	43	83	53	33
	6	6	6	6	6	6	6	6

7.	14	24	64	44	84	54	34	74
	6	6	6	6	6	6	6	6

8.	15	25	45	85	55	35	75	95
	6	6	6	6	6	6	6	6

EXERCISE 112. — WRITTEN EXAMPLES

Add:

	(1)	(2)	(3)	(4)	(5)	(6)	(7)
	2	6	6	6	6	6	6
	3	2	3	5	4	5	6
	4	6	6	5	5	5	6
	5	3	2	6	6	6	6
A.	6	4	6	6	6	5	6

	61	26	36	24	65	43	42
	53	65	45	35	56	54	14
	56	46	61	46	43	66	81
B	64	63	53	65	36	65	25

	304	116	156	65	156	350	125
	36	35	63	264	225	164	81
	125	504	165	56	504	46	307
	13	26	34	64	62	232	210
C.	500	216	326	346	46	65	46

Subtract:

	987	649	832	896	738	683	275
D.	623	606	230	366	612	460	263

	695	979	863	594	720	984	798
E.	462	326	630	32	600	661	566

ADDITION—7'S

EXERCISE 113. — THE COMBINATIONS WITH OBJECTS

1	2	3
7	7	7

4	5	6
7	7	7

ADDITION—7'S

EXERCISE 114. — TABLE

1 + 7 =	6 + 7 =	7 + 1 =	7 + 6 =
2 + 7 =	7 + 7 =	7 + 2 =	7 + 7 =
3 + 7 =	8 + 7 =	7 + 3 =	7 + 8 =
4 + 7 =	9 + 7 =	7 + 4 =	7 + 9 =
5 + 7 =	0 + 7 =	7 + 5 =	7 + 0 =

1. 7 boys and 9 girls are — children.
2. 5 days and 7 days are — days.
3. 7 clocks and 6 clocks are — clocks.
4. 8 chairs and 7 chairs are — chairs.
5. 7 tables and 7 tables are — tables.

6.	7 + 0 =	5 + 7 =	3 + 7 =	7 + 8 =
7.	6 + 7 =	7 + 4 =	0 + 7 =	2 + 7 =
8.	7 + 3 =	8 + 7 =	7 + 1 =	7 + 6 =
9.	7 + 7 =	5 + 7 =	1 + 7 =	7 + 9 =
10.	4 + 7 =	9 + 7 =	5 + 7 =	7 + 2 =

ADDITION—7'S

EXERCISE 115. — THE COMBINATIONS

1. 1 2 3 4 5 6 7 8 9 0
    7 7 7 7 7 7 7 7 7 7

2. 7 7 7 7 7 7 7 7 7 7
    1 2 3 4 5 6 7 8 9 0

3. 5 8 0 2 6 3 9 1 4 7
    7 7 7 7 7 7 7 7 7 7

4. 7 7 7 7 7 7 7 7 7 7
    9 6 8 5 7 4 0 1 3 2

5. 4 7 7 1 7 7 6 7 3 7
    7 2 7 7 3 1 7 4 7 0

6. 9 7 7 5 7 8 0 2 7 7
    7 5 9 7 6 7 7 7 8 5

7. 7 and what other number will make each of these numbers: 15; 12; 9; 7; 10; 13; 8; 16; 11; 14?

ADDITION—7'S

EXERCISE 116. — ORAL PROBLEMS

(1)		(2)	
Houses on left,	8	Cost,	$9
Houses on right,	7	Gain,	$7
Houses,	?	Selling price,	?

(3)		(4)	
Black pigs,	7	Pint cups,	6
White pigs,	7	Quart cups,	7
Pigs,	7	Cups,	?

5. The clock strikes 2. May will come 7 hours later. At what time will she come?

6. Ned gives 7 roses to his sister. He has 5 left. How many roses did he have at first?

7. Kate picks 4 flowers. Ann picks 7 more than Kate. How many does Ann pick?

8. The apple tree is 7 feet high. The peach tree is 6 feet higher. How high is the peach tree?

9. Jack lives 7 blocks from school. Will lives 9 blocks farther away. How many blocks from school does Will live?

10. This box is 7 inches wide. That box is 7 inches wider. How wide is that box?

ADDITION—7'S

EXERCISE 117. — DECREASING NUMBERS OF TWO ORDERS

1. | 1 | 11 | 21 | 61 | 31 | 80 | 50 | 90 |
    | 7 | 7 | 7 | 7 | 7 | 7 | 7 | 7 |

2. | 2 | 12 | 22 | 32 | 13 | 53 | 93 | 43 |
    | 7 | 7 | 7 | 7 | 7 | 7 | 7 | 7 |

3. | 4 | 14 | 24 | 54 | 94 | 44 | 74 | 64 |
    | 7 | 7 | 7 | 7 | 7 | 7 | 7 | 7 |

4. | 5 | 15 | 25 | 95 | 45 | 75 | 65 | 35 |
    | 7 | 7 | 7 | 7 | 7 | 7 | 7 | 7 |

5. | 6 | 16 | 26 | 46 | 76 | 66 | 36 | 86 |
    | 7 | 7 | 7 | 7 | 7 | 7 | 7 | 7 |

6. | 7 | 17 | 27 | 77 | 67 | 37 | 87 | 57 |
    | 7 | 7 | 7 | 7 | 7 | 7 | 7 | 7 |

7. | 8 | 18 | 28 | 68 | 38 | 88 | 58 | 98 |
    | 7 | 7 | 7 | 7 | 7 | 7 | 7 | 7 |

8. | 9 | 19 | 29 | 39 | 89 | 59 | 99 | 49 |
    | 7 | 7 | 7 | 7 | 7 | 7 | 7 | 7 |

ADDITION—7'S

EXERCISE 118. — PROBLEMS (ADDING BY 7'S)

1. There are — boats in this picture and — men in each boat. There are — men in all the boats.

2. If there were 5 such boats, how many men would they all hold?

3. ◯ ◯ ◯ ◯ Each of these balls costs 7¢. All the balls cost — cents.

4. In each box I place 7 marbles. How many marbles do I place in 7 boxes?

5. I have some cans that hold 7 quarts of milk each. How many quarts will 6 cans hold?

6. In one week there are 7 days. How many days are there in 8 weeks?

SUBTRACTION—7'S

EXERCISE 119. — DEVELOPMENT

7 + ? = 8
How many are 8 - 7?

1 + ? = 8
How many are 8 - 1?

7 + ? = 9
How many are 9 - 7?

2 + ? = 9
How many are 9 - 2?

7 + ? = 10
How many are 10 - 7?

3 + ? = 10
How many are 10 - 3?

7 + ? = 11
How many are 11 - 7?

4 + ? = 11
How many are 11 - 4?

7 + ? = 12
How many are 12 - 7?

5 + ? = 12
How many are 12 - 5?

7 + ? = 13
How many are 13 - 7?

6 + ? = 13
How many are 13 - 6?

7 + ? = 14
How many are 14 - 7?

7 + ? = 14
How many are 14 - 7?

7 + ? = 15
How many are 15 - 7?

8 + ? = 15
How many are 15 - 8?

7 + ? = 16
How many are 16 - 7?

9 + ? = 16.
How many are 16 - 9?

SUBTRACTION—7'S

EXERCISE 120. — THE COMBINATIONS

1.   9 10 11 12 13 14 15 16
     7   7   7   7   7   7   7   7

2.   9 10 11 12 13 14 15 16
     2   3   4   5   6   7   8   9

3. 15 12   7 16   8 10 13 11
     7   7   7   7   7   7   7   7

4. 13 16 10 12   7 11 14 15
     6   9   3   5   0   4   7   8

5. 11 15 13 11   8 14 10 12
     7   7   7   4   7   7   7   5

6. 10 16 12 16   9 15 13   8
     3   7   7   9   7   8   6   1

7.   12 - 5 =   13 - 6 =   15 - 7 =   10 - 7 =

8.   16 - 7 =   15 - 8 =   12 - 7 =   14 - 7 =

9.   11 - 4 =   16 - 9 =   11 - 7 =   13 - 7 =

SUBTRACTION—7'S

EXERCISE 121. — ORAL PROBLEMS

(1)		(2)	
Men and women,	15	Cows,	12
Men,	7	Red cows,	7
Women,	?	Cows not red,	?

(3)		(4)	
Pad and book,	16¢	Selling price,	13¢
Book,	7¢	Cost,	7¢
Pad,	?	Gain,	?

5. A window had 9 panes of glass. 7 of them were broken. How many panes were not broken?

6. There were 14 birds in a tree. 7 flew away. How many birds were left?

7. The can holds 16 quarts of milk. I pour out 7 quarts. How many quarts remain?

8. Kate has 15 pencils. 7 are red. The others are black. How many are black?

9. Jack has 13 marbles. Ned has 7 less than that. How many has Ned?

10. Frank buys a pencil for 7 cents. He pays for it with a dime. How much does he get back?

SUBTRACTION—7'S

EXERCISE 122. — DECREASING NUMBERS OF TWO ORDERS

1. 8   18   28   68   88   37   57   77
    7   7   7   7   7   7   7   7

2. 9   19   29   89   10   50   70   90
    7   7   7   7   7   7   7   7

3. 11   21   31   51   71   91   41   61
    7   7   7   7   7   7   7   7

4. 12   22   52   72   92   42   62   82
    7   7   7   7   7   7   7   7

5. 13   23   73   93   43   63   83   33
    7   7   7   7   7   7   7   7

6. 14   24   94   44   64   84   34   54
    7   7   7   7   7   7   7   7

7. 15   25   45   65   85   35   55   75
    7   7   7   7   7   7   7   7

8. 16   26   66   86   36   56   76   96
    7   7   7   7   7   7   7   7

ADDITION AND SUBTRACTION—7'S

EXERCISE 123. — WRITTEN EXAMPLES

Add:

	(1)	(2)	(3)	(4)	(5)	(6)	(7)
	7	7	7	7	3	7	7
	6	7	6	7	7	0	7
	5	6	7	2	4	7	7
	4	5	4	7	7	7	7
A.	3	4	3	6	7	7	7
	67	07	67	43	77	25	43
	70	34	56	77	64	76	84
	77	77	45	52	72	77	28
B.	74	56	34	75	67	57	41
	300	206	343	176	256	134	147
	70	37	60	57	175	76	267
	200	15	172	374	247	357	176
	80	707	254	46	166	25	324
C.	200	27	70	277	137	407	72

Subtract:

	(1)	(2)	(3)	(4)	(5)	(6)	(7)
	958	789	397	968	879	587	940
D.	751	577	177	734	777	570	700
	997	792	897	496	379	989	859
E.	770	722	374	274	172	772	155

ADDITION—8'S

EXERCISE 124. — THE COMBINATIONS WITH OBJECTS

1	2	3
8	8	8

4	5	6
8	8	8

7 / 8

8 / 8

9 / 8

ADDITION—8'S

EXERCISE 125. — TABLE

1 + 8 =	6 + 8 =	8 + 1 =	8 + 6 =
2 + 8 =	7 + 8 =	8 + 2 =	8 + 7 =
3 + 8 =	8 + 8 =	8 + 3 =	8 + 8 =
4 + 8 =	9 + 8 =	8 + 4 =	8 + 9 =
5 + 8 =	0 + 8 =	8 + 5 =	8 + 0 =

1. 8 hours and 8 hours are — hours.

2. 5 years and 8 years are — years.

3. 8 feet and 7 feet are — feet.

4. 6 inches and 8 inches are — inches.

5. 8 quarts and 9 quarts are — quarts.

6.	7 + 8 =	8 + 0 =	8 + 6 =	8 + 8 =
7.	8 + 9 =	8 + 3 =	5 + 8 =	2 + 8 =
8.	8 + 2 =	8 + 4 =	6 + 8 =	0 + 8 =
9.	8 + 5 =	8 + 1 =	3 + 8 =	9 + 8 =
10.	8 + 7 =	4 + 8 =	1 + 8 =	8 + 5 =

ADDITION—8'S

EXERCISE 126. — THE COMBINATIONS

1. | 1 | 2 | 3 | 4 | 5 | 6 | 7 | 8 | 9 | 0 |
    | 8 | 8 | 8 | 8 | 8 | 8 | 8 | 8 | 8 | 8 |

2. | 8 | 8 | 8 | 8 | 8 | 8 | 8 | 8 | 8 | 8 |
    | 1 | 2 | 3 | 4 | 5 | 6 | 7 | 8 | 9 | 0 |

3. | 4 | 7 | 9 | 1 | 5 | 8 | 0 | 2 | 0 | 3 |
    | 8 | 8 | 8 | 8 | 8 | 8 | 8 | 8 | 8 | 8 |

4. | 8 | 8 | 8 | 8 | 8 | 8 | 8 | 8 | 8 | 8 |
    | 2 | 5 | 7 | 0 | 3 | 6 | 9 | 4 | 1 | 8 |

5. | 6 | 8 | 8 | 8 | 2 | 7 | 8 | 0 | 8 | 4 |
    | 8 | 3 | 1 | 8 | 8 | 8 | 5 | 8 | 9 | 8 |

6. | 8 | 8 | 8 | 5 | 8 | 8 | 9 | 3 | 8 | 1 |
    | 0 | 6 | 9 | 8 | 2 | 4 | 8 | 8 | 7 | 8 |

7. 8 and what other number will make each of these numbers: 14; 9; 17; 13; 8; 15; 12; 10; 16; 11?

ADDITION—8'S

EXERCISE 127. — ORAL PROBLEMS

(1)
Rugs sold,	8
Rugs not sold,	9
Rugs,	?

(2)
Money spent,	$8
Money left,	$8
Money at first,	?

(3)
Boys present,	6
Boys absent,	8
Boys,	?

(4)
Balls on table,	7
Balls in bag,	8
Balls,	?

5. The clock strikes 5. What will be the time 8 hours from now?

6. Frank is 9 years old. May is 8 years older. How old is May?

7. The red book is 8 inches wide. The black book is 6 inches wider. How wide is the black book?

8. In each of two nests there are 8 eggs. How many eggs are there in both nests?

9. May has 8 red roses and 7 white ones. How many roses has she?

10. Kate is 8 years old. How old will she be 5 years from now?

ADDITION—8'S

EXERCISE 128. — INCREASING NUMBERS OF TWO ORDERS

	1	11	21	71	41	60	90	30
1.	8	8	8	8	8	8	8	8

	2	12	22	42	13	93	33	83
2.	8	8	8	8	8	8	8	8

	4	14	24	94	34	84	54	74
3.	8	8	8	8	8	8	8	8

	5	15	25	35	85	55	75	45
4.	8	8	8	8	8	8	8	8

	6	16	26	86	56	76	46	66
5.	8	8	8	8	8	8	8	8

	7	17	27	57	77	47	67	97
6.	8	8	8	8	8	8	8	8

	8	18	28	78	48	68	98	38
7.	8	8	8	8	8	8	8	8

	9	19	29	49	69	99	39	89
8.	8	8	8	8	8	8	8	8

MEASUREMENTS

EXERCISE 129. — QUART AND PECK

1 Peck = 8 Quarts

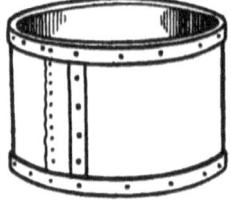 

1. Frank buys 1 peck of apples. How many quarts does he get?

2. For each quart Frank pays 4 cents. How much does the peck of apples cost?

8. One peck of corn costs 25 cents. How much will 4 pecks of corn cost?

4. How many quarts are there in one peck? How many quarts are there in 3 pecks?

5. Mother buys a peck of apples. The children eat 3 quarts of the apples. How many quarts remain?

6. Will picks one peck of apples. May picks 5 quarts of apples. How many quarts do they both pick?

ADDITION—8'S

EXERCISE 130. — PROBLEMS (ADDING BY 8'S)

1. In this picture there are — spiders. Each spider has — legs. All the spiders have — legs.

2. Each spider catches 8 flies. The spiders catch — flies in all.

3. ▯ ▯ ▯ ▯ ▯ In each measure there is one peck of apples. How many quarts are there in all?

4. ◊ ◊ ◊ ◊ If one quart of milk costs 8¢, how much will four quarts cost?

5. In each row there are 8 seats. How many seats are there in six rows?

6. A log was cut into nine pieces. Each piece was 8 feet long. How long was the log?

SUBTRACTION—8'S

EXERCISE 131. — DEVELOPMENT

8 + ? = 9
How many are 9 - 8?

1 + ? = 9
How many are 9 - 1?

8 + ? = 10
How many are 10 - 8?

2 + ? = 10
How many are 10 - 2?

8 + ? = 11
How many are 11 - 8?

3 + ? = 11
How many are 11 - 3?

8 + ? = 12
How many are 12 - 8?

4 + ? = 12
How many are 12 - 4?

8 + ? = 13
How many are 13 - 8?

5 + ? = 13
How many are 13 - 5?

8 + ? = 14
How many are 14 - 8?

6 + ? = 14
How many are 14 - 6?

8 + ? = 15
How many are 15 - 8?

7 + ? = 15
How many are 15 - 7?

8 + ? = 16
How many are 16 - 8?

8 + ? = 16
How many are 16 - 8?

8 + ? = 17
How many are 17 - 8?

9 + ? = 17
How many are 17 - 9?

SUBTRACTION—8'S

EXERCISE 132. — THE COMBINATIONS

1.	10 _8	11 _8	12 _8	13 _8	14 _8	15 _8	16 _8	17 _8
2.	10 _2	11 _3	12 _4	13 _5	14 _6	15 _7	16 _8	17 _9
3.	12 _8	15 _8	17 _8	8 _8	10 _8	13 _8	11 _8	14 _8
4.	14 _6	11 _3	16 _8	17 _9	12 _4	15 _7	13 _5	10 _2
5.	14 _8	11 _8	8 _0	13 _5	17 _8	9 _8	15 _7	9 _1
6.	10 _8	17 _9	15 _8	13 _8	11 _3	12 _8	14 _6	16 _8

7. 12 - 4 =   14 - 8 =   13 - 8 =   17 - 9 =
8. 15 - 7 =   17 - 8 =   11 - 8 =   14 - 6 =
9. 15 - 8 =   12 - 8 =   16 - 8 =   13 - 5 =

SUBTRACTION—8'S

EXERCISE 133. — ORAL PROBLEMS

(1)		(2)	
Chairs,	15	Horses,	17
Black chairs,	8	White horses,	8
Chairs not black,	?	Horses not white,	?

(3)		(4)	
Selling price,	13¢	Selling price,	14¢
Cost,	8¢	Gain,	8¢
Gain,	?	Cost,	?

5. A log is 17 feet long. It is cut into two pieces. One piece is 9 feet long. How long is the other piece?

6. The clock strikes 12. What was the time 8 hours ago?

7. How many quarts are there in 1 peck? A man has 11 quarts of apples. He sells 1 peck of them. How many quarts are left?

8. Ned pays 16¢ for some bread and milk. The bread costs 8¢. How much does the milk cost?

9. May wants to buy a 14-cent book. She has only 6¢. How many more cents does she need?

SUBTRACTION—8'S

EXERCISE 134. — DECREASING NUMBERS OF TWO ORDERS

1.	9 8	19 8	29 8	79 8	99 8	48 8	68 8	38 8
2.	10 8	20 8	90 8	40 8	11 8	31 8	81 8	51 8
3.	12 8	22 8	62 8	32 8	82 8	52 8	72 8	92 8
4.	13 8	23 8	33 8	83 8	53 8	73 8	93 8	43 8
5.	14 8	24 8	84 8	54 8	74 8	94 8	44 8	64 8
6.	15 8	25 8	55 8	75 8	95 8	45 8	65 8	35 8
7.	16 8	26 8	76 8	96 8	46 8	66 8	36 8	86 8
8.	17 8	27 8	97 8	47 8	67 8	37 8	87 8	57 8

ADDITION AND SUBTRACTION—8'S

EXERCISE 135. — WRITTEN EXAMPLES

Add:

	(1)	(2)	(3)	(4)	(5)	(6)	(7)
	8	8	8	8	8	8	8
	7	8	7	6	8	5	8
	6	7	8	8	7	8	8
	5	7	6	5	8	8	8
A.	4	6	8	8	8	8	8
	74	82	87	83	88	78	85
	68	67	56	48	87	84	58
	87	88	48	25	86	68	78
B.	78	84	88	38	84	87	48
	208	588	685	187	268	70	75
	80	85	35	178	87	509	28
	130	107	80	286	353	208	483
	302	48	100	168	188	80	80
C.	56	64	108	76	42	130	88

Subtract:

	(1)	(2)	(3)	(4)	(5)	(6)	(7)
	489	897	999	989	598	858	739
D.	288	485	81	821	380	248	738
	856	489	388	983	687	288	789
E.	32	78	65	70	43	58	24

MEASUREMENTS

EXERCISE 136. — REVIEW

1. How many pints are there in one quart?
2. How many quarts are there in one peck?
3. How many inches are there in one foot?
4. How many half dollars equal a dollar?
5. How many quarters equal a dollar?
6. How many dimes are there in one dollar?
7. How many cents are there in one dime?
8. How many cents are there in a half dollar?
9. How many cents are there in one dollar?
10. How many cents are there in a quarter?
11. How wide is your desk? How long is it?
12. How long is the room? How wide is it?
13. How long is your pencil? Your thumb?
14. How wide is your book? How long is it?
15. How high is your desk? Your chair?
16. It is now VI o'clock. What will be the time 6 hours from now?
17. The time is XI o'clock. What was the time 9 hours ago?

COMPARISONS

EXERCISE 137. — ORAL PROBLEMS

1. Which is more, a pint or a quart? How much more?

2. Which is more, a peck or 9 quarts? How much more?

8. Which is less, a dozen or 8 things? How much less?

4. Which is less, a dozen eggs or 12 eggs?

5. Which is worth more, a nickel or a dime? How much more?

6. Which is worth more, a dime or 7 cents? How much more?

7. Which is the greater number, IV or IX? How much greater?

8. Which is the smaller number, X or VI? How much smaller?

9. Which is longer, a foot or 8 inches? How much longer?

10. Which is longer, a quarter hour or a half hour? How much longer?

11. May is 12 years old. Ann is 8 years old. Which is the older? How much older?

COMPARISONS

12. Jack is 17 years old. Ned is 9 years old. Which is the younger? How much younger?

13. A book costs a dime. A pencil costs 8 cents. Which is worth less? How much less?

14. Will was in school 5 hours. May was in school 3 hours. Which of them was in school the longer? How much longer?

15. Frank leaves school at half-past three. Rose leaves school at quarter-past two. Which of them leaves school the later?

16. One bag holds a peck of corn. Another bag holds 12 quarts of corn. Which bag holds more corn? How much more?

17. A peach tree is 15 feet high. An apple tree is 9 feet high. Which is the higher? How much higher?

18. One box is 18 inches wide. Another box is 9 inches wide. Which box is the wider? How much wider is it?

ADDITION—9'S

EXERCISE 138. — THE COMBINATIONS WITH OBJECTS

1	2	3
9	9	9

4	5	6
9	9	9

7	8	••• ••• •••
9	9	••• ••• •••

ADDITION—9'S

EXERCISE 139. — TABLE

1 + 9 =	6 + 9 =	9 + 1 =	9 + 6 =
2 + 9 =	7 + 9 =	9 + 2 =	9 + 7 =
3 + 9 =	8 + 9 =	9 + 3 =	9 + 8 =
4 + 9=	9 + 9=	9 + 4 =	9 + 9 =
5 + 9 =	0 + 9=	9 + 5 =	9 + 0 =

1. 9 dollars and 9 dollars are — dollars.

2. 7 cents and 9 cents are — cents.

3. 8 trees and 9 trees are — trees.

4. 9 flowers and 5 flowers are — flowers.

5. 6 red roses and 9 white roses are — roses.

6.	9 + 9 =	8 + 9 =	5 + 9 =	9 + 7 =
7.	9 + 5 =	7 + 9 =	0 + 9 =	6 + 9 =
8.	3 + 9 =	9 + 6 =	9 + 1 =	9 + 8 =
9.	9 + 0 =	4 + 9 =	8 + 9 =	9 + 2 =
10.	2 + 9 =	1 + 9 =	9 + 4 =	9 + 3 =

ADDITION—9'S

EXERCISE 140. — THE COMBINATIONS

1. 1 2 3 4 5 6 7 8 9 0
    9 9 9 9 9 9 9 9 9 9

2. 9 9 9 9 9 9 9 9 9 9
    1 2 3 4 5 6 7 8 9 0

3. 7 9 3 2 4 8 1 0 6 5
    9 9 9 9 9 9 9 9 9 9

4. 9 9 9 9 9 9 9 9 9 9
    5 8 6 4 0 2 1 3 2 7

5. 8 9 1 9 6 9 0 9 5 9
    9 2 9 3 9 1 9 7 9 9

6. 9 4 2 9 9 3 9 7 9 8
    0 9 9 4 8 9 6 9 5 9

7. 9 and what other number will make each of these numbet-s: 11; 17; 12; 10; 15; 9; 14; 18; 13; 16?

ADDITION—9'S

EXERCISE 141. — ORAL PROBLEMS

(1)		(2)	
Good peaches,	9	One stick,	8 feet
Bad peaches,	9	Another,	9 feet
Peaches,	?	Both,	?

(3)		(4)	
Selling price,	$6	Spent,	9¢
Loss,	$9	Left,	7¢
Cost,	$?	At first,	?¢

5. There are 9 boys on a ball team. How many boys are on two teams?

6. School begins at 9 o'clock. 3 hours later children go home to dinner. What time is it then?

7. Five years ago Frank was 9 years old. How old is he now?

8. Mr. May pours 6 quarts of milk out of the can. He has 9 quarts left. How much had he at first?

9. To 7 pints of water I add 9 pints. How many pints of water does that make?

10. The clock strikes 2. What will the time be 9 hours from now?

ADDITION—9'S

EXERCISE 142. — DECREASING NUMBERS OF TWO ORDERS

1. | 1 | 11 | 21 | 61 | 91 | 30 | 70 | 40 |
    |---|----|----|----|----|----|----|----|
    | 9 | 9 | 9 | 9 | 9 | 9 | 9 | 9 |

2. | 2 | 12 | 22 | 92 | 13 | 73 | 43 | 83 |
    |---|----|----|----|----|----|----|----|
    | 9 | 9 | 9 | 9 | 9 | 9 | 9 | 9 |

3. | 4 | 14 | 24 | 74 | 44 | 84 | 54 | 64 |
    |---|----|----|----|----|----|----|----|
    | 9 | 9 | 9 | 9 | 9 | 9 | 9 | 9 |

4. | 5 | 15 | 25 | 45 | 85 | 55 | 65 | 95 |
    |---|----|----|----|----|----|----|----|
    | 9 | 9 | 9 | 9 | 9 | 9 | 9 | 9 |

5. | 6 | 16 | 26 | 86 | 56 | 66 | 96 | 36 |
    |---|----|----|----|----|----|----|----|
    | 9 | 9 | 9 | 9 | 9 | 9 | 9 | 9 |

6. | 7 | 17 | 27 | 57 | 67 | 97 | 37 | 77 |
    |---|----|----|----|----|----|----|----|
    | 9 | 9 | 9 | 9 | 9 | 9 | 9 | 9 |

7. | 8 | 18 | 28 | 68 | 98 | 38 | 78 | 48 |
    |---|----|----|----|----|----|----|----|
    | 9 | 9 | 9 | 9 | 9 | 9 | 9 | 9 |

8. | 9 | 19 | 29 | 99 | 39 | 79 | 49 | 89 |
    |---|----|----|----|----|----|----|----|
    | 9 | 9 | 9 | 9 | 9 | 9 | 9 | 9 |

ADDITION—9'S

EXERCISE 143. — PROBLEMS (ADDING BY 9'S)

1. There are — boys playing ball, — boys watching them, and — boys running away. There are — boys in all.

2. Six schools have ball teams. On each team there are 9 boys. How many boys are on the six teams?

3. 🍞🍞🍞🍞 How much will these loaves of bread cost at 9¢ each?

4. 📦📦📦📦📦 How many marbles can you place in these boxes if you place 9 marbles in each box?

6. A quart of apples costs 9 cents. How much will seven quarts cost?

SUBTRACTION—9'S

EXERCISE 144. — DEVELOPMENT

9 + ? = 10
How many are 10 - 9?

2 + ? = 11
How many are 11 - 2?

9 + ? = 11
How many are 11 - 9?

3 + ? = 12
How many are 12 - 3?

9 + ? = 12
How many are 12 - 9?

4 + ? = 13
How many are 13 - 4?

9 + ? = 13
How many are 13 - 9?

5 + ? = 14
How many are 14 - 5?

9 + ? = 14
How many are 14 - 9?

6 + ? = 15
How many are 15 - 6?

9 + ? = 15
How many are 15 - 9?

7 + ? = 16
How many are 16 - 7?

9 + ? = 16
How many are 16 - 9?

8 + ? = 17
How many are 17 - 8?

9 + ? = 17
How many are 17 - 9?

9 + ? = 18
How many are 18 - 9?

9 + ? = 18
How many are 18 - 9?

1 + ? = 10
How many are 10 - 1?

SUBTRACTION—9'S

EXERCISE 145. — THE COMBINATIONS

1.   11 12 13 14 15 16 17 18
     9   9   9   9   9   9   9   9

2.   11 12 13 14 15 16 17 18
     2   3   4   5   6   7   8   9

3.   15 12 18 16 11 14 13 17
     9   9   9   9   9   9   9   9

4.   18 14 17 13 16 12 15 11
     9   5   8   4   7   3   6   2

5.   10 10 13 15 14 12 16   9
     9   1   9   6   9   3   7   9

6.   13 16 17 18 12 14 15 17
     4   9   8   9   9   5   9   9

7.   17 - 9 =   13 - 4 =   16 - 7 =   16 - 9 =

8.   13 - 9 =   17 - 8 =   15 - 6 =   18 - 9 =

9.   14 - 9 =   15 - 9 =   14 - 5 =   12 - 9 =

SUBTRACTION—9'S

EXERCISE 146. — ORAL PROBLEMS

(1)
Apples and peaches,	18
Apples,	9
Peaches,	?

(2)
Hat and coat,	$17
Hat,	$9
Coat,	$?

(3)
Cost,	14¢
Loss,	9¢
Selling price,	?¢

(4)
Had,	16¢
Spent,	9¢
Left,	?¢

5. A log is 17 feet long. A piece 9 feet long is cut off. How many feet remain?

6. The clock strikes 11. How many hours ago did it strike 2?

7. May is 18 years old. Ned is 9 years old. Which is the older? How much older?

8. One box is 1 foot wide. Another box is 9 inches wide. Which box is the wider? How much?

9. Jack stands 15 feet from a tree. Ned stands 9 feet from the tree. Which of them is nearer the tree? How much nearer?

10. Ned is 9 years old. In how many more years will he be 13 years old?

SUBTRACTION—9'S

EXERCISE 147. — DECREASING NUMBERS OF TWO ORDERS

1.
10	20	60	30	80	59	79	49
9	9	9	9	9	9	9	9

2.
11	21	31	81	12	72	42	92
9	9	9	9	9	9	9	9

3.
13	23	53	73	43	93	63	33
9	9	9	9	9	9	9	9

4.
14	24	74	44	94	64	84	54
9	9	9	9	9	9	9	9

5.
15	25	45	95	65	85	55	35
9	9	9	9	9	9	9	9

6.
16	26	96	66	86	56	36	76
9	9	9	9	9	9	9	9

7.
17	27	67	87	57	37	77	47
9	9	9	9	9	9	9	9

8.
18	28	88	58	38	78	48	98
9	9	9	9	9	9	9	9

ADDITION AND SUBTRACTION—9'S

EXERCISE 148. — WRITTEN EXAMPLES

Add:

	(1)	(2)	(3)	(4)	(5)	(6)	(7)
	9	9	9	9	4	9	9
	8	7	6	2	9	9	9
	7	5	3	9	5	9	9
	6	4	5	3	9	5	9
A.	5	6	9	9	9	9	9

	(1)	(2)	(3)	(4)	(5)	(6)	(7)
	95	95	98	76	34	89	98
	79	89	46	99	95	97	49
	93	78	73	49	29	59	97
B.	89	95	99	92	69	99	29

	(1)	(2)	(3)	(4)	(5)	(6)	(7)
	209	99	67	199	605	30	209
	59	37	58	97	63	309	106
	367	95	299	59	59	90	209
	199	487	49	198	92	408	307
C.	19	193	309	79	89	69	108

Subtract:

	(1)	(2)	(3)	(4)	(5)	(6)	(7)
	998	597	958	493	609	947	399
D.	903	293	912	290	305	923	304

	(1)	(2)	(3)	(4)	(5)	(6)	(7)
	493	367	875	258	599	797	988
E.	90	52	63	44	96	93	75

ADDITION

EXERCISE 149. — WRITTEN PROBLEMS

(1)		(2)	
Cows,	25	1 peck,	28¢
Horses,	18	1 peck,	28¢
Sheep,	37	1 peck,	28¢
Animals,	?	3 pecks,	?¢

3. In each room there are 48 seats. How many seats are there in 4 rooms?

4. A man pays $98 for a horse and $46 for a wagon. How much do they both cost?

6. In a school there were 89 children. 27 more came. How many children were then in school?

6. Kate pays 47 cents for meat, 24 cents for bread, 15 cents for milk, and 20 cents for apples. How much does she pay for all?

7. A man buys four horses. Each horse costs f98. How much does he pay for the horses?

8. A man pays $59 for a wagon. He sells it at a gain of $25. For how much does he sell it?

9. Kate is 24 years old. Her father is 39 years older. How old is her father?

10. A man buys books for $14, chairs for $27, and a table for $39. How much does he spend?

ADDITION

11. In five rooms in a school there are 46 boys, 37 girls, 50 girls, 42 boys, and 38 girls. How many children are there in the five rooms?

12. In five lots a man has 87, 36, 61, 79, and 50 sheep. How many sheep has he?

13. A log was.cut into three pieces. The pieces were 10 feet, 19 feet, and 24 feet long. How long was the log?

14. Frank is 19 years old. How old will he be 27 years from now?

16. A tree is 59 feet high. Another tree is 38 feet higher. How high is the other tree?

16. Mr. May buys a wagon for $75. He has left. How much had he at first?

17. In a school there are 98 children present. 32 children are absent. How many children belong to the school?

SUBTRACTION

EXERCISE 150. — WRITTEN PROBLEMS

(1)		(2)	
In car,	97 men	Books in store,	98
Went out,	25 men	Books sold,	73
Left in car,	? men	Books not sold	?

3. Will had 84 cents. He gave 23 cents to his brother. How much had he left?

4. A pole was 75 feet long. It was broken into two pieces. One piece was 32 feet long. How long was the other piece?

6. A man had 85 horses. He sold 13 of them. How many horses did he have left?

6. There were 76 apples in a box. 34 of them were sold. How many were left?

7. A man had $75. He paid $55 for a wagon. How many dollars did he have left?

8. A table costs $47. I wish to buy it. I have only $25. How much more do I need?

9. Mr. More is 87 years old. Mr. May is 52 years old. How much older is Mr. More than Mr. May?

SUBTRACTION

10. In a school there are 87 children. 42 are boys. The others are girls. How many are girls?

11. One pole is 67 feet long. Another pole is 53 feet long. How much longer is the first pole than the second pole?

12. May has 36 roses. Ann has 32 pinks. Which has more flowers? How many more?

13. Kate's father is 47 years old. Her mother is 37 years old. How much younger is the mother than the father?

14. Will has 36 inches of string. Ned has 49 inches of string. Which has the longer piece? How much longer?

16. May is now 13 years old. In how many more years will she be 27 years old?

16. Which is the larger number, 86 or 98? How much larger?

17. Mr. Frank is now 58 years old. How old was he 32 years ago?

ADDITION AND SUBTRACTION

EXERCISE 151. — WRITTEN PROBLEMS

1. There are 49 boys in a class. One day 16 of them were absent. How many were present?

2. I paid $34 for a wagon. I sold it at a gain of $16. For how much did I sell it?

3. A pole is 77 feet long. 25 feet are under water. How much is above water?

4. 28 children left school. 89 children remained in school. How many were there in school at first?

6. A grocer had 89 pecks of apples. He sold 47 pecks. How many pecks remained?

6. In a class there are 56 boys, in another 38 girls, in another 47 boys. How many children are there in the three classes?

7. Rob is 27 years old. His father is 39 years older. How old is his father?

8. Ned cuts a pole into five pieces. Each piece is 17 feet long. How long is the pole?

9. Ned is 10 years old. In how many more years will he be 59 years old?

ADDITION AND SUBTRACTION

10. Mother buys some bread and some meat for 89 cents. The bread costs 24 cents. How much does the meat cost?

11. A horse cost $98. A wagon cost $35. Which cost more? How much more?

12. An apple tree is 27 feet high. A pine tree is 59 feet higher. How high is the pine tree?

13. A house is 25 feet wide. It is 58 feet long. How much longer is it than wide?

14. A table and a chair cost $65. The table cost $45. How much did the chair cost?

15. In three cars there are 36, 58, and 90 men. How many are there in all?

16. John picks 40 apples. A dozen of them are not good. How many are good?

17. One quart of apples costs 4 cents. How much does a peck of apples cost?

18. May's mother is 48 years old. May is 35 years younger. How old is May?

ADDITION

EXERCISE 152. — REVIEW: FUNDAMENTAL COMBINATIONS

	3	9	6	8	7	3	2	6	3	5
1.	5	7	4	3	7	6	2	8	4	9
	7	6	7	4	0	4	6	7	9	6
2.	4	9	8	5	0	4	7	3	2	5
	2	4	9	5	6	2	5	4	3	5
3.	5	8	4	7	2	8	8	9	2	5
	9	7	7	2	9	5	3	8	6	3
4.	6	5	2	9	5	3	8	6	3	3
	8	8	4	7	5	6	4	8	3	4
5.	5	8	6	9	4	6	7	4	7	2
	2	5	9	2	8	2	3	8	8	9
6.	6	6	9	7	9	4	9	2	7	8
	5	4	6	8	7	6	5	4	2	7
7.	2	3	7	5	2	3	4	2	3	6
	3	4	7	6	5	4	3	2	9	4
8.	2	9	9	2	3	4	8	2	3	7

SUBTRACTION

EXERCISE 153. — REVIEW: FUNDAMENTAL COMBAINTIONS

1. 18   11   15   12   16   10   13   17
    −9   −3   −7   −4   −8   −3   −6   −8

2.   9   7   4   2   8   6   7   5
    −5   −3   −1   −0   −4   −5   −2   −3

3. 15   8   11   6   12   4   13   8
    −9   −5   −9   −6   −6   −3   −5   −2

4.   5   12   5   14   7   13   9   10
    −2   −5   −4   −7   −4   −4   −7   −8

5. 13   8   10   16   9   11   8   15
    −7   −8   −9   −7   −3   −6   −0   −6

6.   5   13   7   4   10   11   11   9
    −5   −9   −7   −2   −4   −4   −2   −0

7.   1   3   8   9   6   14   5   7
    −0   −2   −3   −6   −0   −8   −1   −5

8. 17   15   12   10   14   11   10   14
    −9   −8   −3   −7   −6   −8   −5   −9

VOCABULARY

PART I

a	does	how	Ned	sheep
and	dog		nine	six
Ann	drink	I	now	sold
apple		In		
are	eat		of	the
	eight	Jack	one	then
book		Jill		there
bring	five		pig	they
buy	four	leaf	pint	three
		leaves	play	to
can	give	lot		two
cat			quart	
come	has	man		water
cop	have	many	see	we
cow	he	May	sell	with
	her	me	seven	
did	him	more	she	you

PART II

absent	black	children	eighty	forty
add	boat	cost	eleven	from
aesk	both	cot		front
all	box	count	fare	
along	boy		father	gave
an	bread	date	feet	get
another	by	day	fifteen	girl
as		dime	fifty	glass
at	cake	do	figure	
away	came	dot	find	had
	car	dozen	first	hand
back	caU		flew	here
be	cent	each	foorteen	high
big	chair	egg	foot	higher
bird	change	eighteen	for	his

hold	money	pear	seventy	tiain
hoose	mother	pele	shorter	top
horse	Mr.	pencil	side	tree
	much	piece	sise	twelve
if		place	sister	twenty
inch	name	plant	sixteen	
into	need	plate	sixty	use
is	nest	pleaad	small	
it	next	pot	some	wagon
	nickel	present	step	walk
Kate	nineteen		stick	wall
	ninety	rale	street	was
large	number	ran	string	were
late		read	strip	what
left	oar	receive	subtract	which
leg	off	red	such	white
length	old	remain	sum	wide
less	older	ride		Will
let	on	Rob	table	will
line	or	room	take	window
little	other	rope	taken	wish
loaf	owe	Rose	ten	worth
long		rose	than	write
longer	pad	row	that	
	paid		them	year
make	pail	same	these	younger
marble	pan	school	thing	your
may	pane	second	thirteen	
melon	paper	seed	thirty	
milk	pay	seventeen	this	

PART III

above			picture	stand
ago	farmer	larger	pin	store
amount	farther	last	pine	strike
animal	finger	later	pink	
	flies	live	playing	team
bag	flower	loaves	pour	third
ball	fly	log	price	thumb
banana	fourth	loss		time
belong	Frank		quarter	together
block	fruit	measure		took
broken		meat	remained	
brother	gain	men	right	under
	good	must	Roman	
called	greater		rug	want
catch	grocer	nearer	running	watching
class	gun	new		way
clock		not	seat	week
coat	half		selling	went
corn	halves	o'clock	shall	wider
	hat	only	show	women
dark	home	out	sixth	would
dinner	hour		smaller	writing
dollar		past	so	
draw	jack	peach	spend	
		peck	spent	
equal	kind	pick	spider	

www.ingramcontent.com/pod-product-compliance
Lightning Source LLC
Chambersburg PA
CBHW020415080526
44584CB00014B/1334

The Feedstore Chronicles

Travis Erwin

THE FEEDSTORE CHRONICLES Copyright © 2011 by Travis Erwin

All rights reserved. Printed in the United States of America. No part of this book may be used or reproduced in any manner whatsoever without written permission except in the case of brief quotations embodied in critical articles or reviews.

This narrative is created solely from the author's memories. Names, characters, businesses, organizations, places, events and incidents either are the product of the author's imagination or are used fictitiously. Any resemblance to actual persons, living or dead, events, or locales is entirely coincidental.

For information contact; Barbadum Books

Address PO Box 39992 Amarillo, TX, 79120

www.BarbadumBooks.com

Cover design by LoudMouth Tooley

Cover Photo by Alex Keto

ISBN: 978-1-934606-32-2

Second Edition: November 2016

10 9 8 7 6 5 4 3 2